THE HOLISTIC ENTREPRENEUR

JODENE SHAER

HOW TO SUCCEED

BY FOCUSSING ON SELF-WORTH, INTUITION, AND HAPPINESS.

CONTENTS

This version published in South Africa

ISBN: 978-0-620-74500-0

Book Design by: Putty Perfect Publishing

FOREWORD

One does not often come across a book that invites you to walk a path that indirectly asks that you self-reflect, take time for deep introspection and leaves you with a hunger to seek out and carve an expedition for your own life, one that leads you to the best you. This intriguing story, told by the holistic entrepreneur, our very own Jodene Shaer, is a riveting, real and raw account of not only her life, but an echo into our own lives as entrepreneurs.

Not only have I had the privilege of knowing Jodene through my work as an activist, social entrepreneur and the Executive Director of Miss Earth South Africa, but I have come to know this inspiring South African on a personal level too. Jodene is no stranger to the South African social media scene, in fact that is where it all started. I fell in love with her campaign #FollowSA, a concept that put her way above the pack. Jodene was ahead of the game when many of us were just getting to understand this life-altering world of social media.

It came to me as no surprise that Jo would jump into the deep end and allow her book to come to life, a book of passion and experience. I avidly watched from a distance as she shared the up's and down's of putting this masterpiece together through her online posts. It is evident that this book shares moments and memories of her journey that speak directly to a quote from the book that reads as follows: "The other side of relationships within business is one of intuitively and instinctively selecting people who you can be human with." I have had that opportunity, and count Jodene as a precious being to be human with.

For those who have not yet met Jodene in person, her most magnificent rendition of how she has mastered making the most delicious lemonade out of life's lemons, is not only visible on a daily basis through her posts on social media, but through this beautiful book which unpacks the stories behind many of her learnings, trials and tribulations. I read every page of this book and could relate, and I almost heard my subconscious talking to me through Jodene's shared wisdom and insight as an entrepreneur.

Truly grateful to have had the opportunity to read this book before the world, there is no doubt that this book will be one of those game changers for every reader, fan and the thousands of friends who will share the lessons between the covers, over wine or even at the book club. Jodene has given us the DIY guide to handling life's greatest challenges in business, as a brave warrior who must choose not to live only in 'survival mode' but to choose to thrive. I was captivated and inspired by the narration, which is an invitation to be brave and allow the universe to bring back what I put out there.

Thank you, Jo, for your time and labour of love in putting 'The Holistic Entrepreneur' together. Herein you leave a legacy... we are forever thankful...

Dear Reader... may this book make you aware that there is indeed a 'Holistic Entrepreneur' in us all. It is for us to deliberately put into action the carefully laid out steps and mindful decisions that this brave woman has shared as she has reached a place of bliss, because instead of doing what she was good at, she started doing what made her happy!!!

A lesson for us all.

Catherine Constantinides

International Climate Change Activist & Humanitarian @ChangeAgentSA

WELCOME TO THE HOLISTIC ENTREPRENEUR

"The Universe rewards bravery!" – Me

While my friends were marrying off their Barbie to Ken, mine had turned her plastic mansion into an international business empire. Although life sometimes has a thrilling resemblance, my story hasn't exactly panned out to look much like my childhood fantasies. For most of us, our grand youthful visions of our lives have been massively watered down by the gallons of grown-up realities we face daily. My playground never made space for financial struggle, rejection, emotional turmoil, low self-esteem and my office building burning down while playing with my dreams.

Yes, that happened. In August 2004, while shopping with a friend, the hysteria in my mother's call ripped away any desire to be an entrepreneur that day, the building was on fire. I remember the feeling of claustrophobia, while driving and watching the smoke billowing from my family home at least eight kilometres away, where my business was located. The closer I got, the more the sky blackened and the less I felt prepared for what life had handed me. Forensics concluded a faulty wire was the silent culprit. Unbeknown to firefighters, there were oxygen tanks in the house because my father was an emphysema sufferer. What was supposed to be a contained fire, ended up being a blast of destruction that blew windows out of apartment buildings two blocks away. As the flames hit the oxygen tanks, the fire turned into a raging inferno.

The fire only burned one curtain in my home-based wellness salon, but the eleven fire trucks had pumped enough water into the building to drown my business. As dramatic as it may sound, four years into having my own business, that was the day I stopped doing what I was good at and started striving to do what made me happy.

For most of us wanting to grow and learn, the vast amount of ever-available business advice has answered many questions, except the one we most need an answer to: How do you manage to do what makes you happy, despite the realities of life and business? The reality is, we give up on following our passion to earn a living. Some have succeeded in making the transition from giving up on what's considered 'a stable career' to following their purpose. This should have guaranteed happiness. However, many slog away, burning the candle at both ends, as every self-made entrepreneur says you should. There are often many personal sacrifices. You are saying 'no' to time with friends more often than 'yes' because you can't financially match their financial ability to have fun, but you're doing what you dreamed of - so why is it turmoil and struggle?

Have you noticed that the toughest financial times are when we hope that the right business course or book will patch the sinking ship carrying our dreams? Many try and even more will find the money to throw at self-help for any glimmer of a solution. The reality is we've been handed down an oversimplified idea of manifestation and an over complicated version of success. What does that mean? It's not about focusing on the positive. It's about focusing on the truth. Look at what the law of attraction claims to offer, if you keep focusing on the positive.

What are they describing as the 'workable formula'? Focus on the good, even if the bad is throwing daily warnings that you're denying yourself the bravery to look at what's not working. Does anyone tell you that hidden behind the false happiness is your undiscovered potential? What would take your business to new heights? In other words, the more motivational memes you surround yourself with, the less you tell yourself the truth about where you actually are in your life, and it's usually further along than your low self-esteem allows you to acknowledge.

That's not how manifestation works. That's setting yourself up for losing faith in your Universe, your choices, your business and yourself. If it were a fail-proof way, the self-help industry wouldn't be worth billions of dollars. According to ABC news in May 2015, "One mega-seller", Stephen Covey's, "The Seven Habits of Highly Effective People", is so massively popular that it gave rise to a publicly traded corporation. Last year, Franklin Covey, who is in the business of providing "integrated training and performance -enhancement solutions to organisations and individuals," recorded sales of $333 million".

What does this say about us? Instead of trusting our intuition, we have lost the connection to self and throw the little time and money we have at hopeful solutions from external sources. Do you not have the will to succeed? Are you not capable and deserving of having everything? I believe you are. Unfortunately, those aren't the parts of yourself you're encouraged to upskill. The milestones to success are far more internal, emotional and conscious than we have been taught. The real power behind entrepreneurship is about discovering our most authentic self. It is about unlocking the ultimate life purpose behind our service offering and reaping the financial rewards through nurturing our self-esteem and having a loving relationship with money. Yes, love.

You must have a plan. That's the rule to getting anywhere in life. In high school, you already had to know who you wanted to be so you could choose the related subjects to get you into the university or college you desire. Or, you choose the subjects your elders think you should take, while praising you for the brilliant corporate mogul you will become. "What do you want to be when you grow up?" was my least favourite question, because I didn't have a realistic answer.

I scraped through school because I missed the point of needing anything besides basics math, reading and writing. I dealt my parents the horrid task of having to raise a daydreamer. My seemingly flighty ways gave everyone the impression that I would amount to nothing, so they began treating me that way. I was viewed as the girl who would scrape by as an adult. My family labelled me as irresponsible, to the point of not entrusting me with fetching a bowl from the kitchen without assuming I would return with the wrong one.

I believed them, so when it came time to finish school and choose a career, I was still undecided, and my mother chose for me. I kid you not. With love, she sent me to secretarial college, and everyone hoped for the best. Thanks to my mom, I found something I loved and went from being dropped in grades to passing high school, to finishing third in my year and being hired as a personal assistant by the principal, without an interview. I loved my job for the first eight months, because I had a boss who really wanted to be a nurse and her compassion oozed while nurturing me into the corporate world.

When she left to pursue her dream, I was introduced to the other side of the dog-eat- dog, cutthroat corporate world. Reality struck when my new boss forced me to lie about a document she forgot to send, which had serious repercussion. It was back in the days of fax paper and Tippex, where mistakes could be cut out and forged, along with your integrity. I felt sorry for my parents, when I told them it was wiser to resign immediately after swearing at my boss. Once again, I didn't know what I wanted to be when I grew up, but from that experience I certainly knew I wasn't happy being employed.

I wanted to be an entrepreneur and I wanted to love what made me money. If you're anything like me, you've read dozens of books, some of them written by millionaires who forgot to mention the sleepless nights of fear and angst. Some of them prefer to gloss over the fact that they had a leg up along the way. I too turned to self -help books, plagued with the assumption that we know what we want in our lives, because everyone is supposed to have a plan. I'm here to tell you that you can be a success without having a plan. In the peak of the 'law of attraction' hype, it was all about dreaming beyond your wildest imagination. Even Oprah bought into it, celebrating her larger -than-life achievements by rewarding her audience with elaborate gifts they surely could have only manifested through the universal law of abundance.

Vision boards are the biggest red flag to throwing people like me off course. I was one of the exaggerated dreamers, whose first vision board had a private yacht on it. Why not, right? You dream it, keep positive about it and you will surely manifest it? Never mind the fact that if I stand on a docked cruise liner, the size of a small hotel, I get seasick. No one told us that if you can't define the purpose behind your choices, your goals won't become a reality.

Today, I'm the co -owner of two successful businesses, brimming with opportunity in a time when the world is struggling a recession. Dinner conversations with friends centre on the lack of potential clients and non–existent budgets. I've learned my lessons, with two failed businesses as the treacherous teachers of what has become the cornerstones to my two successful ones. None of what I learned ended up coming from external sources, with the exception of a metaphysics course I took in July 2004.

Have you been paying attention? Does that date sound familiar? That's right, it was at a time when my day spa couldn't afford cotton wool and my recruitment agency for the wellness industry couldn't pay the phone bill, the fire struck my business. With the building in flames, I hysterically called my metaphysics teacher, who came dashing over to stand by my side. In the next moment, she helped me change my life forever. Holding my hand, she said, "you have five minutes to cry and feel desperately sorry for yourself and then you're going to tell me why this is the best thing that could have happened to you".

From that day on, I paid attention. I patiently worked at figuring out the link between choosing to study metaphysics and the timing between setting my intentions, the fire and the slow realisations of what it meant to live the life of a holistic entrepreneur. I'm telling my story to reassure you that your daydreams have the potential to be your flourishing reality.

As my story unfolds through the book, you'll see that you are already fully equipped with all the business tools you need, if you commit yourself to trusting the process and doing the work. It's nearly twenty years down the line and I consciously give myself the full attention I require to remain focused, within integrity and in the 'manifestation zone'. I've had wins and losses, continued failures and successes, made the right choices and the wrong ones, but my foundation has been solid, because of the time I've spent cementing my self-worth into my reality.

I may have the story to tell, but ultimately, you are going to help yourself. I'll share the tools to building self-esteem and self -worth, visualising your dreams into reality, intuitively choosing what's best for your business and building wealth by making friends with money. What you won't find is textbook business solutions; how to draw up five year plans, or, when to hire and fire. The practical business tools in this book are clearly aimed at working from a place of purpose, because while others were making textbook decisions, I was imagining, redefining my faith and making time for happiness and fun.

I can't promise you a magic formula; I don't believe that being wildly successful has anything to do with aiming your business at the Fortune 500 list. This book doesn't guarantee that you'll be a millionaire, but I can promise you that whatever life throws at you, you'll know you can take it and my wish is that you'll do something profoundly empowering with it.

HOW TO USE THIS BOOK

The Holistic Entrepreneur is written for anyone who has a vision of achieving something worthwhile for themselves. Each one of us is an entrepreneur, because we are all striving to create something. Entrepreneurs are described as people who grab new ideas and action them into opportunities. If you're sitting in an office and don't see the opportunity within your job, but you're craving to find time to do a craft, then yes, you're an entrepreneur. There is a constant commentary on the lack of numbers of women in the boardroom or men who are least likely to be employed, when the reality is entrepreneurship has the potential to be far more rewarding for both. It's for the young corporate who wants the desk by the window and his private office on the top floor, the mom who wants to make her way in the world, while freely having time to tuck her kids into bed at night, the artist who refuses to be starving and the girl who never wants to grow up on her way up the success ladder.

These are some suggestions on how to use this book to its fullest potential.

Create Time

Not having time is our way of protecting ourselves from the fear of the unknown. I know, because I never had time. Now I wake up with the sunrise - without the help of an alarm clock - and give myself the "me" time I need. Whether it's a few hours a day, week or month - commit. We'll chat about it more in the book but mark your 'time off' in your diary as a crucial appointment, because in essence, it is.

Make Space

You're going to need to be still, be quiet, write and dance around a bit ... I kid you not! So, make space to do this. While getting back on my feet from business failures, I moved back with my mother and the only private space I had was standing in the shower, but it was mine. To this day, despite having my own home, I still find sanctuary in my shower time. Make sure you can close the world out for a while and don't hide the book or the process from anyone so that you can freely ask for help or time if it's needed. Yep, that's another thing we'll be tackling because no one was meant to do this living thing on their own.

Your Journal

Some days it's tough to remember the very powerful part of your personality you discovered a few days ago, so nothing goes unwritten. Your journal will be the personal life support you keep close at hand for when life throws you the unexpected, which as we know, will happen a lot. Each year I take advantage of the post-Christmas sales and buy a new journal and pen to see me through the year. It spends the year next to my bed and has everything from teardrops to doodles and the odd page torn out in frustration or fear - but it's there when I forget what I remembered about myself.

Pin it

Whether it's in the inside of your cupboard or for the world to see, you are going to need a pin board. If you can't afford it now, buy or bum some sticky notes to plaster on a wall or door. I'm not telling you what we'll be doing with that just yet, but get ready!

Imagination

It's a thing I made up because that's the essence of visualising and affirming. To reassure you, I've never done a course in breathing, my mind never shuts up while I'm trying to meditate, and personal beliefs aren't linked to the process at all. I'll reveal the necessity for micro-imagining and breathing before we get started, but you'll be doing your fair share of it.

Have Fun

If you're not having fun in the process, STOP! Don't quit, but realise that you're fully entitled to throw the book in a drawer. Make sure it's one you have to dig in at least twice a year.

Before we dive headfirst into the world of The Holistic Entrepreneur, let's test the waters with the first exercise.

Get comfortable, either sitting or lying down and close your eyes for no more than two minutes. Take a deep breath in and then out, a few times until you feel ready to begin imagining the first time you went to the funfair and the rides looked super scary, but you did it anyway. If you've never been on the rides, think of something scary but fun, which you can relate to and recall the sensation of the fun you had while screaming your lungs out and feeling fear hit the pit of your stomach on the ride.

I would suggest that when you have your journal, you do this imagining again and describe the sensation as a start to sensing the difference between having fun and being afraid or having an awful time and instinctively knowing it's time to bail.

1

ESTEEM VS. THE SABOTEUR

Do you know the difference between self-worth and self-esteem? Before you instinctively Google, let's do it the old fashioned way and begin with a story.

"Once upon a time there was a grand oak tree that stood steadfast in the woods for hundreds of years. During the warm summer, it blossomed with acorns and leaves, bursting with an array of green shades. In the winter, however, it was baron and looked as if it may not weather another storm. Beaten from the snow and broken from the angry wind, the tree relied on its tireless roots to hold it steady and waited for the warmth of summer so it could begin to heal and blossom once again."

Unbeknown to us, we have the same endurance as the oak tree because we also have roots that anchor us through any storm. It's called our self-worth. Through the brutality of life and unimaginable obstacles, our self -worth has the ability to guide us through any storm as long as we identify the roots of our steadfast personality.

The part of us that take the beatings, which falls apart and carries the scars of life is the self-esteem. Our esteem is meant to shift between emotions and push through the extremes of life. We were born to grow from fear, joy, sadness, excitement, hurt and all the emotions in between.

This is why it's so important to lay a solid foundation. It doesn't matter how spectacular the architecture may be, if the groundwork is unstable, the structure is sure to come tumbling down. You've read a few books from successful entrepreneurs and keep up with blog posts from motivational businessmen and women, so you're equipped to forge forward on the solid footing of entrepreneurship, right? I thought so too, but a couple of failed businesses forced me to reassess the type of foundation I had created.

With the self-help I was relying on, I had ticked all the boxes from having an accountant, to solid admin systems, and I was really good at what I did, but with every passing month I was more in debt. Our instinct is to think it's business stuff, like not being skilled enough, so we do an online course of some sort. When that doesn't work, we clock more personal hours and equate the time spent away from our business as the reason we're struggling through it, so we upskill some more. We use money we don't have as a desperate attempt to figure out what we're "getting wrong".

After flunking out of corporate – with a few swear words thrown at my boss for good measure – I joined my mother in her established beauty college. Truth is, she strong-armed me when the ship sank. Really, I was booked for a cruise soon after I quit corporate and the cruise ship sank two days before I was supposed to leave. I hadn't even unpacked when my parents saw the red flag to a future nobody, so I was summoned back to my mother's office to make use of my secretarial skills. I can be organised, so I did that. I also bore easily, so I did that too.

For my sanity, my favourite pastime became hanging out with the students while they were on a break. We were about the same age and they were more fun than filing, so my mother let me be. What no one knew was this was the turning point from my aimless career.

My mother had hired a part-time, retired business lecturer and the students hated her. It wasn't what she was teaching, but that she was old and making a boring subject even more unbearable. So, I started using their breaks to bring the fun into studying business. Within a few months, the students begged my mother to let me teach them instead. I was excited about the new challenge, which was perfectly timed with figuring out that I wanted a far more exciting career than what secretarial work could offer me. Truthfully, being told what to do wasn't going to work for me either. I was twenty years old when life gave me a glimmer of what my passion may have been: teaching. This was an ideal way to have the best of both worlds, because no one else in the family wanted to take over the business, no matter how established it was.

Within a year, I had recreated the curriculum and developed the simple business management assignment into a ten -month project that resulted in a business plan ready to present to a bank. I was thriving and my mother's legacy grew closer to becoming mine. Eventually, I went on to set and mark exams for the national governing board of the beauty industry and they implemented my business project into the greater syllabus.

To my dismay, within a few years I was back to uncertainty and craved a new challenge, so I began studying all the modules of beauty therapy. I hated waxing, I loved massage, tolerated facials and couldn't paint fingernails to save my life, so I opted to teach everything instead.

I was restless. There was something missing, despite being promoted to deputy principal and having my future paved for me, I wasn't happy. Honestly, the business may have been a picture of success on the outside, but behind closed doors it was a pile of debt and bad business management. Sorry mom! It wasn't an overnight decision and the thought of letting her down kept me stuck for a few more years. I felt selfish and ungrateful for a life set out for me and I turned on my personality by blaming my aimless nature. It's not hard to look back on the past and pinpoint the negative traits. I didn't know what I wanted to do when I was younger, and I didn't know what I wanted to do then either. Direction wasn't a strongpoint for me, so I labelled it as a poor personality trait and stuck through it for years, trying to change my personality.

By that time my mother had already handed the running of the business to me and had moved onto hiring beauty therapists and hairstylists for international cruise liners. In an exciting twist of fate, the beauty lecturers and I were eventually upskilled to train the new sea recruits on treatments that hadn't hit the South African shores yet. The excitement of this new world confirmed my fears and I knew I couldn't take over my mother's business.

Five years down the line, I still hadn't changed my mind, was desperately miserable and turned on myself for being selfish and aimless. Despite not wanting to carry the legacy, and not being able to let my family down, I compromised and in 1999 while still teaching and running the college, I opened one of the first Day Spas in the country with one of the other teachers. We took the international treatments we had learned and introduced the likes of hot stone massage and Lomi- Lomi Hawaiian massage into the services and with that, my first business was born. We were flying and won The Best of Joburg award in 2001. We had the best products, services and were ahead of our time. But within two years I was feeling as incomplete at the spa as I had been while running the college.

Once again, I turned on my aimlessness and repeated the cycle of blame and more self-hate. Instead of stepping back and seeing the positive that may have been trying to rear its' head in my personality, I covered it with shame. In an attempt to keep some part of me happy, I opted to study further and extended my treatments to holistic therapies, which I thrived in.

My greatest frustration as a holistic healer was having a client come to a treatment with a "fix me" attitude. Between chakra balancing, crystal healing, Reiki and healing massage, everyone held out for a quick fix to happiness and I became the "go-to girl". While I was stuck behind closed doors, expecting to make magic, my clients were turning to the flood of self-help books hitting the shelves. Law of attraction, affirmations, vision boards and manifestation were the word on the street and during treatments I tried desperately to get my clients to take some personal responsibility in the process.

I was equally lost and masked my frustrations by turning to the same formulas everyone else was. I read the books and delved into every aspect of self-help that I could. I would lock myself away for the weekend and listen to tapes on how to manifest abundance. My mirrors were plastered with post-it notes that had affirmations like, "I am a success magnet and I attract success in whatever I do" and "Being happy comes easy to me. Happiness is my second nature". To heal my perceived aimless ways, I said the affirmation, "My life is on track and I am abundantly happy in it". Well, wasn't that the farthest from the truth?

Manifesting affirmations is supposedly easy. Stand in front of the mirror and repeat the same affirmation daily, with positivity and conviction. The law of attraction is then meant to kick into motion and what we affirm should become our reality. What made it abundantly worse was the Oprah movement of people sitting on her couch and sharing stories of their visualisations manifested into reality and their affirmations coming to life. I was most frustrated because I began my hunt to understand the universe when I was as young as six years old and over twenty-five years later, I felt just as naive.

As manifestation went, I had managed to live up to my vision of being an entrepreneur, despite being broke and desperately unhappy. Everything else I was affirming hadn't turned into reality and the frustration from getting it so wrong perpetuated more self-doubt and less belief in the law of attraction. By that time, I felt I had no right to offer the healing modalities and became obsessed with attempting to unravel my ingrained traits and reinvent myself as a more focused, grateful person.

The depression broke me, and I became an obese recluse, spending days eating and listening to anything related to understanding the law of attraction. I read books I hated, while stuffing my face to keep me focused, because I had convinced myself that I flunked out of everything and an incomplete book was not an option. My teachers, siblings and parents were all right about me from the youngest age. I was unfocused and wouldn't amount to much.

By the time I was thirty, I had unravelled and was desperate to find happiness of any kind. I blamed my weight, broken relationships, tragic losses and family drama for my misery, which included my financially struggling businesses. Yet, there was something within me that wouldn't give up the search for a happy, successful, confident me. It was the tiniest glimmer of self-love, but it was strong enough to pull me out of my dark home and into therapy. Now that I embrace my unconventional personality, I get why I knew mainstream psychology wasn't going to crack this nut. Instead, I went the holistic route and started sessions with a counsellor who mastered tarot, numerology, astrology and archetypes to name a few. I chose her because, through it all, I still believed in the tools from the universe and wanted to understand why they weren't working for me, like Oprah said they should. It was time to start concentrating on my roots, and not the greenery of my leaves.

Contrary to what I call, "the positivity movement", the law of attraction only works if you are living within your truth. This can only be possible if your roots are steadfast enough to weather the storm as you shift in the direction of that truth. That means we can't go any further until you've found your roots of self-worth. This process took me a few years, but now it's one of the first projects I give to anyone who is mentored by me. Yes, it's so fundamental that it's a project and may take a few days to complete. I suggest finishing it before you read the rest of the chapter. Give yourself a deadline of five days, including a weekend, because you're going to need some time with a few people who know you well.

Rooted within your personality are strengths that are

waiting to root you firmly for the rest of your life. They are purely positive traits that you've unconsciously relied on in your darkest moments. Although you may know a few of them, there are strong parts of yourself that others may admire too and between you and your people, you're going to create Your SELF WORTH LIST.

You don't need to be in a good space to do this, so don't put it off if you're having a low day. I created mine when I was so broke that I couldn't take my friends to coffee and chat about my qualities. Take some quiet time and think about highlights of both lows and highs in your life and what YOU KNOW about yourself. Don't find a quality and then knock it down because you remember a time when you didn't rise to the occasion. That is going to be the default thought, because your roots aren't firm yet. When I began my list, I was clutching at straws, but I realised that my fighting spirit for both my business and I showed my determination, vision for what I wanted in my life, never-give-up attitude and resilience.

After asking my best friend and my mother, the roots of my self-worth started to positively surprise me. Even though I was dragging myself out of the depths of negativity, they saw qualities of an unwavering faith, passion, uncanny ability to make anything happen, innovation and a positive attitude when none seemed to be found. Seriously?! While I felt broken and desperate, those closest to me were inspired by my fighting spirit.

I never would have discovered those elements of worth without their input and neither will you. Ask them to make their own list and don't you dare take anything off it. It doesn't matter how long the list is,

but it can't be less than twenty steadfast character traits. You're going to need them to weather the bravery of true manifestation.

Once the list is complete, make a few copies and stick them on the inside of cupboards, in your diary, make it your screensaver... as long as you can turn to it when the storm moves in and your self-esteem is taking a beating. My original list is in a battered old plastic sleeve and still goes with me everywhere in my laptop bag, years down the line.

Now this part is important: If the process of creating the list or the list itself gets you down, don't worry, that's what the rest of this chapter is for. In the meantime, just make it visible.

With the backup of our self-worth to rely on, we create a safer space to delve deeper into our personality and uncover the hidden traits that the positivity movement has kept us from discovering. Carl Jung, the Swiss psychotherapist who founded analytical psychology, called this part of us, "our shadow". He introduced us to the unconscious aspect of ourselves, which the conscious ego doesn't recognise in itself. Allow me to give you my spin on this very complex theory. Each of us has two parts, the ego and the soul. Both parts have the same fundamental purpose, to unconditionally love and push us towards what's best for us. The soul knows we are meant to be fearless in life and pushes us in the direction of risk taking, boldness and willingness to experience the array of emotions life has to offer. Our soul knows we need to experience loss and failure, but it also endeavours to reassure us that we'll come out the other side a much wiser and successful individual.

Our ego is on the same loving quest as the soul, except it doesn't want us to get hurt or feel disappointment. It's the over-protective guardian in our personality and doesn't mind if you never take a risk, as long as you don't experience pain. That's why ego gets the bad rep of being arrogant or defensive. Those are ideal traits for a fearful person trying to avoid failure.

That part of you who wants to protect you from trying and failing or dreaming too big is lurking in the shadows. According to Jung, it is your saboteur and is the greatest divide between you and your potential to create thoughts into things. You know your saboteur already because you trip yourself up all the time with it, but let's take a moment to officially meet it.

Grab your notebook and complete this sentence, "Every time I enthusiastically tackle a project, life ..."

My sentence goes like this, "Every time I enthusiastically tackle a project, life becomes so busy that I have put it on hold." A perfect example is writing this book, which has taken about four years. Time became my enemy and no matter how much I said I wanted to; I was so busy building my business that I completely convinced myself that focusing on my passion (writing) would be detrimental.

We are always challenged by our ego and the protective default that allows our saboteur to step into the light. New Age self-help has been no help at all, with the constant encouragement to only focus on the "positive". The more we do that, the less chance we have of truly getting to know what our ego and saboteur does in times of fear and then we blame life's circumstances.

Our saboteur doesn't do just that. Trust me, there are way more obstacles we put in the way and lay blame to life, like needing the money we saved up to

unexpectedly fix the car or having to cancel the meeting because the babysitter let you down.

There's no quick fix in this process, so continue this exercise daily and try pinpointing how that incident could be self-sabotage to keep you safe from your fears. Remember, the more you convince yourself it's life's fault and you couldn't help it, the deeper into the shadows you hide your saboteur.

The saboteur is a tricky one because it's carrying out the unconscious messages your ego is sending it - the loving, safer messages to protect you from failure. It certainly has been protecting you from the backlash of going against the conventional business books by telling you to focus more on your self-worth than your financial wealth. Only for so long can the saboteur unconsciously allow us to stagnate, before the soul pushes back and causes a longing we usually label as depression.

'You're powerful, but you're not THAT powerful!'

Stick that up somewhere as a constant reminder that the law of attraction is real, but you don't get to determine the path life is going to take you on to get you there.

Only the conscious survive the journey between visualising a dream and turning it into reality and the most conscious approach you can take is getting to know yourself.

Here's a theory. What if we're being misguided? According to the Urban Dictionary, The Law of Attraction is a New Age belief based on the concept that "like attracts like" and that by focusing on positive thoughts, such as affirming to yourself that you will win a million dollars, your thoughts and affirmations will subsequently manifest themselves by granting you the one million dollars. Your thoughts are similar to magnets. Positive thoughts will attract positive outcomes and vice versa for negative thoughts.

Let's play devil's advocate, shall we? Have you stopped to ponder why we can't scroll through our Facebook Timeline or have a meltdown with a friend without a regurgitated positivity quote slapped in our face? Don't you wonder why all this positivity engulfs us, yet the world seems more chaotic than ever before? We know millions of people are doing daily abundance affirmations, but we're drowning in economic debt. The visualisations of finding love and happiness certainly haven't improved the state of relationships and where are those daydreamers whose vision boards reflect Branson-type wealth? What if the happiness movement tries to instil in us to always remain positive, because like attracts like, but the true universal law urges us to tell ourselves the truth and face our unhappiness?

I'm way more worthy than my current manifestations reflect, and I guarantee, you are too. If manifestation is so easy, why don't we have what we positively say we want? Don't tell me you focused on having the limited happiness you're surrounded by. It's an assumption, I know, but none of us really believe the people around us choose a mediocre life, when the gurus tell us we can have whatever we imagine. I certainly am not living what I imagine daily, or I would have been published years ago and writing a second or third book from my cabin in the mountains. Even in my purely abundant moments, when I look at my success and happiness, it's far from the picture I painted for myself.

Don't get me wrong, I completely believe in the law of attraction and as the chapters unfold, I'll share all I've manifested and confess why the rest of my dreams are taking longer, but first we have to admit that there's something fundamentally wrong with the manifestation teachings. The tragedy is in giving up on ourselves because the "New Age" law of attraction have failed us.

If you've ever focused your intention on creating anything in your life, then you've sparked the universal law of attraction into action. On that day when you blew out your birthday candles and whispered a secret longing wish, or threw your arms in the air and wondered why your life is where it is, you woke up the innermost part of you and didn't even realise it.

So, if you've planned, wished and daydreamed, why doesn't your life reflect the picture in your head? You didn't believe in yourself enough - that's why. There are no multiple-choice options here. That's it. We simply don't have enough self-belief to carry through on our vision.

Listen up! You can manifest anything you want, no matter how outrageously unattainable it may seem, only if you believe in yourself. It doesn't matter how much faith you have, be it religious, spiritual or logical. The clichés about self- love are all true, except for the part where it magically appears. There's no fairy godmother to wave her wand or genie that can wish away your financial fears. It takes hard work and that has nothing to do with the hours you'll put into your business. These are the focused moments you commit to discovering who you are and what truly makes you happy and in turn, abundant. Don't say you know it already, or you certainly wouldn't have had the desire to read this book.

There is a story I was told in my early teens, by a rabbi who was a fundamental part of my early search for the meaning of life. He told me about an old man who thought he had wisdom because of his age and his faith. One day the floods came, and the old man knew that his god would save him. The water rose high and a friend came to the house to tell him rescuers were there to help, but the old man told his friend his god would save him. The house filled with water and the man went to sit on the roof, waiting to be saved and very much in faith. His friend returned in a boat and begged the man to get in, but he whole heartedly believed that if he kept praying and believing, he would be saved. Holding onto the highest tree branch, the old man's friend returned and told him no one was left to come back and save him if he didn't climb in the boat, but the man believed he would be saved in the form of a miracle. The boat did not come back and the old man drowned. When he met with his god, he asked, "why didn't you save me? I believed in you the way I had been told my whole life and when I needed you most, you were not there." His god replied, "I sent someone to save you three times, but you didn't get in the boat."

This story doesn't have anything to do with a religious faith, but it has a powerful message about the responsibility we have to take in our own lives. The world is filled with methods and tools that are supposed to help us figure out our lives, but in the end, success and happiness is completely dependent on ourselves.

I had no clue that tackling my relationship with me would be the formula to digging myself out of the failing businesses I never truly wanted and creating the businesses I'm so passionate about today. It's wildly mind- blowing that I never imagined my current career when taking the first conscious step to finding happiness. Without realising it, I was throwing the conventional manuals of business away and opening myself up to the holistic world of abundance and prosperity.

In this chapter, you have met both the self-worth that you've brought into the light and the saboteur hiding in the shadows. Being aware that the two are constantly battling every decision you need to make, will create an awareness that is ground-breaking in your journey. Before moving on, here's a micro-imagination to help you befriend both sides of yourself.

In your quiet space, where you won't have any disturbances, do a 5-minute visualisation, starting with seeing yourself as the strong oak tree. Imagine your roots deeply embedded in the earth and feel the confidence that nothing will be able to uproot you. If you can, name some of the self-worth aspects on your list as confirmation. Each time you do this, you will be

able to name more. Then move your attention to the tree above the ground and imagine the saboteur causing treacherous conditions, while you take a beating. Take deep breaths and exhale calm and confidence, in the direction of the raging saboteur, thinking about what it does to trip you up. Once again, the more you do this, the more you will remember how the saboteur plays out. In that space of calm, your saboteur and self -worth have a chance to meet and your worth will grow in confidence, while your saboteur will slowly become the guardian instead of the raging warrior.

I have been doing this visualisation for well over a decade and on my lowest days I go outside and lean against a tree for the additional reminder. Do this whenever you feel you're in sabotage mode, which is going to be often, I assure you.

2

GOALS VS. PURPOSE

Entrepreneurship is gaining popularity and thanks to the coming of age of the handful of millennial millionaires, almost everyone wants to be one. However, the limited number of successful entrepreneurs will prove that it's not as easy as flunking out of school and becoming a success like Richard Branson. Thinking you can do a better job than your boss and having a gut feeling that the clients will follow you or developing an app that you know will knock Snapchat off the grid does not guarantee success. We've been told that success is measured by the amount of money in your bank account - and you want a lot of it. There seem to be two distinct types of entrepreneurs in recent years: the younger, aspiring entrepreneurs wanting the big bucks for not doing much and the older generation of hopeful entrepreneurs who are happy with making just enough, while burning the candle at both ends. But both of those scenarios are just tragic!

I blame the bombardment of articles, written by any old Joe Soap, about the ten steps to successful entrepreneurship or the five characteristics of a successful entrepreneur.

When we are confident and making money, these articles may not impact us, but in the moments of vulnerability, when that month-end looms and you know the call from the bank is coming, there's a desperate search for solutions. We turn outwards and find ourselves trawling the Internet for solutions and relying on Google to help us find the pathways to better entrepreneurship. Hands up if you haven't read an article defining the characteristics of a successful entrepreneur when in a financial bind? No one? That's what I thought.

A few months back I was invited to talk about brand strategy in the social media space to the final year students at a marketing college. After three years of studies, they had the opportunity to ask me anything about social media strategy, but all they wanted to know was how long it took for me to start making money. At another speaking engagement, where I addressed about a hundred aspiring young entrepreneurs on the topic of innovative entrepreneurship, I was fuelled with the same line of questioning. When does the money start to flow? Entrepreneurs are supposed to have wealth and freedom, aren't we? Yes, we are, but if you're going into entrepreneurship for those two reasons then best you get a day job.

In the talk to the aspiring entrepreneurs, a young man stood up and questioned me about research into my competitors, and my lack thereof. That's because I didn't and to this day, I haven't. I threw the question back at him and asked him how knowing what my competitors were doing would impact me if I was doing what I love and not taking my eye off my vision to worry about theirs. His responses were textbook, but everyone knows that the theory and the practical are worlds apart. The discussion turned into a heated argument and eventually the MC stepped in to calm the angered young man down. My point, which pushed him over the edge, was telling him to let go of the textbook approach to success and to turn his focus inward to discovering what he's most passionate about.

I asked him what he wants to offer the world and he told me what he thought the world needed. The more he told me that he wanted to know if the world wanted what he had to offer, the more I told him the world won't know they need it until he shows them what it is. A few days later, I got hold of the organisers and asked them if they could get a message to the young entrepreneur and let him know I wanted to spend some quality time with him, explaining the holistic approach to entrepreneurship, to which he declined. I couldn't blame him, but I was saddened not to be able to empathise with him, because the messaging to entrepreneurs is so contradictory. On the one hand, we are told that passion is the key to success and then we're told to do market research to see if anyone needs what we are passionate about. We are encouraged to create money by doing what we love but then we are forced to fit that into the outcome of market research.

You can't break passion down into a business plan - trust me, I've tried. To truly merge the world of passion and financial freedom, you have to feel it and let your passion guide you, and to get that right you have to throw away the textbook and trust that what you have to offer is both unique and needed.

In 2009 I bought myself out of the spa and recruitment agency by paying off fifty percent of the debt and leaving my ex-business partner to eventually dissolve them both. I borrowed money from my mother and although it was a financially traumatic time, the relief was far greater, and I was ready to embark on that which I was passionate about. By that time, I had finished my metaphysics studies which helped me gain better insight into why we need to overcome obstacles. I learnt everything happens for a reason, understanding the law of attraction and knowing yourself, makes you less of a victim when difficult or challenging things happen, and gives you an opportunity to grow from it. My mother's college was long dissolved and so was my connection to the beauty industry. Yet my yearning to teach never faded and I approached my best friend to partner with me in a business, which would take our metaphysical approach to life and business to corporates.

Greg and I met through a mutual friend, and after sifting past what he loves to refer to as "my drama", we connected on a deeply refreshing outlook to life. I went on to teach and he was part of my first group of students while I was still under the guidance of my teacher. Both he and I blossomed as we uncovered more about ourselves and the mysteries of life. Greg comes from a corporate background, which will make for some interesting stories in the chapters to follow. After teaching together on weekends and working hard to develop our service offering, he took the plunge and left corporate to join me full time in our business. With sketchy direction, we gave birth to Lifeology, a people development business with the slogan, "Courage, Consciousness and a Sense of Humour". We didn't arrive at the name or the defining slogan lightly and we were clear on the services we wanted to offer.

I carried the baggage of two failed businesses and Greg took the dive from the corporate world, we focused on the skills we lacked and searched for business guidance. Our first meetings as partners were with brand strategists and marketing experts who we entrusted with our capital in exchange for business guidance that would safeguard us against failure. However, there was a very apparent problem. Our slogan was all wrong. If we wanted corporates to take us seriously, we had to come up with something less fluffy than telling them to have a sense of humour.

The breaking down of our vision continued with suggestions to align ourselves more with the business world and forget our crazy notion that we could dress down, never make a cold call or spend one cent on advertising. Like skittles, one by one the advisors gave up on us and we poured money down the drain because we were unconsciously going against the very essence of what we wanted to teach the world - that finding our individuality in the world would be our foundation to success.

We developed this cornerstone of Lifeology through Carl Jung's theory of the Collective Unconscious, which refers to the unconscious part of the mind shared among the same species. It's simplified by the phenomenon known as the hundredth monkey effect. Over a thirty-year period, starting in the 1950's, scientists studied the Japanese Snow

Monkey by giving them sweet potatoes on the island of Kosima. Although they thoroughly enjoyed the potatoes, they weren't thrilled about the crunch of the sandy coating. One baby monkey, however, had a plan. She figured out that she could wash the sweet potato in the ocean. She, in turn, taught the young ones around her, who shared this with their parents and close to end of the 1950's all of the monkeys on the Island were washing their sweet potatoes. That's the partially fascinating part. The real proof of the existence of a collective thought among species came at the point where the assumed number of a hundred monkeys were all washing their sweet potatoes on one Island, when reports started to emerge of the identical species of monkeys instinctively washing their sweet potatoes on islands across the seas.

The same applies to any collective, including that of a nation, a race, instinctive mothering and in our case, the collective of the entrepreneur. The hidden mystery of the collective is finding our individuality while remaining a part of that collective. It's easy to spot the ones who are on the right path because they are usually labelled the 'rebel'. Once again, the conflict is perpetuated for the entrepreneur, who is encouraged to find their individuality, but stay within the confines of what it means to emerge as a successful businessperson - and a cloned version of Steve Jobs does not count.

What I'm telling you to do is stop looking outward for what it means to be an entrepreneur and don't subject yourself to the brushstroke characteristics preached by every entrepreneurial magazine. I used to be obsessed with living up to the ideal version of an entrepreneur and went as far as doing an extreme trail run, lugging my overweight body through one of the toughest mountainous terrains in my radius because an article pointed out the focused fitness regime of an entrepreneur. There was no new client waiting for me at the top of that mountain pass and there wasn't one waiting for me at the end of any of the other articles I poured through in the cobweb of entrepreneurial advice. If you want this bad enough, you're going to have to rebel up and do it your way. There's no quick fix exercise for you, but having your self- worth list close by and the courage to do it your way, are the first few steps in the right direction.

Remember the post-it notes we discussed in the last chapter? Well it's time to whip some out and write, "I'm doing it my way" on a few of them. Stick them up on mirrors around your home, in your sun visor in the car or make this statement your screensaver, because having the bravery to go within and trust yourself is about to become real.

Less than a year into the business, Greg and I started to wonder if we had perhaps been wrong and should have taken some of the traditional business advice we were given. We spent months working on defining our service offering and I branched into creating a product called, "manifestation myths". From the small evening courses, we had managed to get off the ground, I was determined to help people have a more realistic approach to manifesting and the law of attraction. All around me, I watched first-hand and saw the destruction people were heading into by thinking it was simple enough to stick up a picture of a car or holiday home and it would magically appear. The reality is a little more complicated than that.

In my early days of teaching, a thirty–something- year- old student, Sue, began the metaphysics course because she felt everything was crumbling around her and getting to know herself better had become a priority. She was unhappily married with two young kids and although she hadn't been happy in her marriage for a while, her unhappiness was getting progressively worse. She started the course because financial issues had crept into their lives and her reliance on her husband was giving him more control and causing greater strain on the marriage. We dug deep to get to the root of the positive that was waiting to be discovered through the chaos, but things only worsened for her, to the point where she started to doubt her marriage and she became desperate to get everything back to the way it was. Even taking time to do the course was angering him and she blamed the course and she blamed me for worsening her situation. We eventually took time to work back to before the course had begun and I asked her what she wished for.

> ***In the still of the night, when you think no one is listening, what do you wish for? Stop! Write that question in your journal and leave it until the end of the chapter.***

Sue gave me her list of goals but that wasn't what I asked for. Remember the ego and soul you met in the first chapter? Do you remember that ego wants to keep you safe, but soul is bursting for you to make a change/take charge and discover your purpose? Your ego is therefore goal-driven, and your soul is purpose driven. I know, she didn't get it either! Picture this. A young boy is sent to soccer practice, because that's what boys should do. He's indoors far too much and spends too many hours doodling on paper and the walls, so he must be bored. He's given a ball and the coach points to the net and tells the boy to kick the ball into the net so he can score a goal. That's the point of the game, after all. Much to the dismay of everyone around him, the little boy wants to know why? What's the point of scoring the goal? Well, to win, of course!

The only problem is, he doesn't want to win because he doesn't want to play. His soul has other plans which are much more purposeful. He wants to draw and bring his imaginary world to life, but he's taught from a young age that his purpose is messy and time wasting, so he obeys his coach and learns to kick the ball into the goal. It's a simple enough exercise and seeing as though he's not allowed to do what he loves; he distracts himself with the goal and becomes a brilliant football player. This doesn't mean he's happy and his memories of scribbling on the walls are long forgotten until one day when he's exhausted and frustrated with life. The success hasn't fulfilled him, and he feels resentment towards the world, but he doesn't know why - because he's learned to be goal driven and he's reaching those goals. One day he snaps and decides he hates the sport, the life and the attention. He then whispers to himself, "I just want to shut the world out and scribble for a while."

A few weeks later he breaks his leg and can never play football again. At this point, his ego could take control and he may shift his goals into another aspect of the sport, like coaching. If not immediately, his soul will yearn until he eventually rediscovers the artist within and lives his purpose. The longer it takes, the more chaos he seems to attract.

Sue eventually told me about her love for Shamanic healing and how she dreamed of owning a healing centre, but she had become a fulltime mom and had given up on the dream years ago. Her goals were filled with happy family activities and her husband wasn't supportive of her vision, so she let it go. Yet, when they fought, she kept throwing it in his face that she let her dreams go for him and their family. What a terrible thing to say, she thought, so she suppressed her dreams even further. Sue grew unhappier and her marriage took strain, so I encouraged her to at least research doing a course in Shamanic healing. Her eyes lit up at the idea, but her husband said no and pointed out all the mothering and wifely duties she had. He reminded her that he paid the bills and that wouldn't be one of them. There were financial struggles already, so Sue let the dream go, again. The course ended but we kept in touch and within a year she contacted me to say her husband filed for divorce and she was forced to work, so she found a job in a holistic store and she got to study some courses for free through them. One of them was a Shamanic course.

We are always guided by our purpose, whether we consciously know it or not. For some people, it's a simple life and for others it's worldly dreams. Either way, our goals are not our purpose and self-help keep us stuck with every reminder to do anything to get there. Unless it's your ambition to become a world-class football player and it fulfils your soul purpose, then aim for the goal. If not, find your purpose! You may very well be clear on your purpose already, but the obstacles in your way seem to tempt you off course, just like mine were doing, so this isn't about doubting what you are passionate about. It's about discovering whether your passion is goal or purpose driven. In my beauty industry days, as much as I loved teaching the business management, or found my calling doing the holistic healing, I was still aiming for the predetermined goal of taking over my mother's business. My true passion trickled through and the search for my purpose led me to where I already was - teaching.

It took me years to figure out that I could create my own style of teaching and not follow anyone else's formula and the more I fought it, the greater the obstacles became. I was at my lowest point, financially, spiritually and emotionally, when the cornerstone of Lifeology's teaching material was developed. Today, Greg uses it for massive scale change management contracts and here I am sharing it with you.

Wherever you are along your career path of making money from your passion, here is an exercise that is going to serve you well. The conflict between ego and soul is constant and knowing whether we are aiming for goals or living our purpose is swayed by our esteem. When I was struggling financially, I would question my greatest passion but when I was making the bucks I felt right on track. Then a downward spiral would hit, and the cycle of confusion would begin again. At my low points, I relied heavily on my memories of success and added those as additional roots to my self-worth list. It's time to do the same.

Turn to your journal landscape and make markings

from the first time you remember having a high or low point in your life. Mine begins at the age of six, when I questioned my parents on our belief system. They weren't angry with me. Instead, they took it far too lightly and teased me about it for years. A high point came soon after, when my grandmother told me the brightest star in the sky was mine and staring at stars is still fundamental in my life. I hated school, so the majority of it is a low point, except for the peaks of joy like loving teaching my teddy bears in order to make school bearable. There were low points of losing grandparents and my family home being auctioned off when I was sixteen.

Then the high of excelling in secretarial and a low again of surviving just a few months in the corporate world. Continue to plot the highs and lows, don't ask anyone else what they remember and don't ponder on it for hours. Take a trip down memory lane and grab the memories that flow to you. Once that's done, for each memory, ask yourself what you learned about yourself and how that character trait is serving your higher purpose. Make notes of each point, because it's going to become important when you start to uncover more of your purpose and stretch your bravery into your business.

I've written this chapter in immense empathy, remembering the waves of depression that kicked in while looking at the world around me and seeing everyone on track in their lives, while I felt so off the beaten path. Even when I was doing what I loved, money was a struggle, the clients weren't knocking on my door and I developed a hatred for any form of self-help that told me to have a goal. After plotting my timeline, knowing my self-worth and discovering my purpose, I wasn't much closer to feeling as though I was truly living. I wasn't abundant but I knew I wanted to be. If you have a clear business idea, you're in a great place, and if it's feeling like your passion then you're in an even better place. If you don't have a clear business idea, but you've got a dream, then you're in a great place too and if you don't have a vision or a plan but you know you can't do what you've been doing and you have to do something different, then welcome aboard because you're also in a fantastic space

> ***Quick, grab your journal again and turn to a blank page. In the centre of it, draw a circle the size of a walnut and write "ME" inside it. Then around the circle write, "I'm the centre of the universe!" You see all that empty space around you? That's called endless possibility.***

This limited part of you has a name. It's called your Highest Esteem. It's the part of you that will discover a newfound bravery from one challenge and want you to push further onto the next challenge. Have you ever saved up for a trip or your first piece of art? In the beginning, you had a purpose to save and your ultimate reward would be what you envisioned. Did you stop there? Neither did I. As soon I realised I could attain one level of business success, I immediately reached for another and then another and before long I was doing things in my business, I never dreamed I was capable of. I began with a bad track record of business decisions, so in the beginning, I made none of them.

Greg was tolerant of my insecurities but eventually he started to push back. Not because he was tired of me, but because he could see glimmers of my esteem and he knew that pushing me out of my comfort zone would be beneficial to the business. I accused him of relinquishing responsibility, purely because I was afraid of my unknown abilities, but he pushed me to make decisions for the business.

At one point, I was ready to quit the partnership because he left me to negotiate a difficult client's contract renewal. I felt abandoned by him, but I was also determined to maintain an outstanding level of service to the client. I sobbed in fear and made two major errors in the negotiation contract, which I blamed him for, but the client accepted the terms and was happy for me to adjust the contract after explaining my oversights. The one mistake was a miscalculation in the monthly retainer, where I had undercharged them. They settled on the higher fee and I felt my esteem want to reach further.

Today, I'm solely responsible for negotiating new clients for our social media agency, Chat Factory, and it thrills me to the core. My Highest Esteem is now craving more, like maybe our first international client. Why not?

It's time for you to meet your Highest Esteem in a micro-imagination. Close your eyes and get comfortable by focusing on your breathing and concentrating on the air flowing in and out of your body. Once you are relaxed, imagine yourself walking through a hall of mirrors. Some will distort you; some will shrink you; some will make you laugh. You stroll around and find yourself standing in front of a lone mirror, that doesn't make your look different, but it makes you feel different.

Your reflection looks wildly confident and extremely brave. Your perfect posture indicates brimming success and you see a hunger for more in your eyes. You have no clue what has sparked this reflection and that is perfectly okay because you're simply going to revel in the feeling. Stare at this abundantly successful

reflection of yourself and take note of yearning for even more. Feel the "knowing" that there is more to come, to create an even greater reflection of your highest esteem.

I have been doing this visualisation for nearly two decades and whatever I achieve, my Highest Esteem reflects more. It thrills me and drives me, but in the very beginning, it simply kept me brave enough to face another day. If you're broken, merely allow your Highest Esteem to feel fixed in the slightest way and I assure you something will shift. Make note of what happens, even if it's a smile from a stranger when you feel invisible in the world. Striving for success can be daunting but not feeling as though you are destined for it, is potentially disastrous. You are...so awaken that part of yourself that knows it.

Remember that question, "in the still of the night, when you think no one is listening, what do you wish for"? It's time to start taking note of what you hear yourself think and feel. You don't have to take any action, because the book is filled with that. Just listen to your silent wishes, frustrated grumbles, what makes you sigh in a moment and journal your thoughts. Keep them safe and let's see what becomes of it.

3

BUSINESS PLAN VS. HAPPINESS PLAN

"Don't feel guilty if you don't know what you want to do with your life. The most interesting people I know didn't know at twenty two what they wanted to do with their lives, some of the most interesting forty year olds I know still don't". Baz Luhrmann said that in his, spoken word song 'Everybody's Free to Wear Sunscreen', in 1999.

The contradiction between living life for the moment and having a plan has the potential to be financially and emotionally destroying to the entrepreneur. We are constantly steered in the direction of creating a business model because we can't walk into a bank and say, "it's my life purpose, believe me, it's going to be a success". It's a pity because the whole economy could benefit from that approach.

For those of us who are more emotionally attached to our business, it's usually tougher to put our dreams onto paper, but we do it anyway. They usually emerge as a vision board because it has been drummed into us that you have to have a plan to get to where you're going. Waking up with an action plan (just for today) and a dream, doesn't cut it according to the world. If you've conformed to steering your business in the direction of your business plan and it's working, you're one of the very lucky ones. For the rest of us, if we don't do something different, we are going to lose faith in ourselves and our dreams, then the only thing left to do is throw away the business plan and the vision board.

Follow my lead if you must, but make sure you do it with all safety precautions in place, because I burned mine. Yep, a raging fire consumed the monstrous A1 size vision board that had begun as a symbol of all I dreamed of and ended up being a material reflection of what I thought I wanted. If I had followed the business plan, we were strong-armed into creating by business adviser number two, I would have missed some of the greatest business adventures of my life. Don't throw away your dreams though. Hold tight to those, because you have the potential to become one of the few entrepreneurs who becomes abundantly successful by living their dreams.

Not everyone manages to get it right - no matter how amazing the dream is or how focused you think you are to hold on for the crazy, scary bits of the entrepreneurial ride. Martin was one of those big dreamers and he had a dream I was thrilled to help him reach. Soon after completing a course with me, he admitted his unhappiness in the corporate world and wanted to fulfil his dream of being a natural born chef. He had a cooking style unmatched for someone who had never done a course or been taught culinary skills.

One day, Martin found himself a retrenched, single guy. He lived the simple life of a bachelor, with a few commitments and was primed to take any life risk he wanted to. This was definitely his time to dream big and he set about creating his plan and his vision to cook in people's homes for parties and events. He mocked up some dishes, which didn't take him long and put together some menus of his unique food combinations. There was nothing traditional about Martin's cooking and he would combine anything from fish and banana to creating sweet battered rose petals. He had done the math and knew how many dinners he had to do in order to cover his costs. Turning his passion into his career took careful planning, to include adding his dreams of freedom to cook whenever and wherever he wanted.

By the time Martin's retrenchment happened, he had a fair amount of his unique recipes to start approaching individuals and event companies, and he began his new business with a clear plan and much enthusiasm. One by one, people showed their unwillingness to try new things and turned down Martin's menus, but at the same time they showed him the types of food they believed people wanted to eat. They were boring and he knew it. Friends started to encourage him to sell his food at flea markets and fairs, but that wasn't part of his plan, so he pushed on.

Eventually he agreed to showcase his food at a flea market. I popped by to visit and was thrilled to see him all set up and people sampling his outrageous combinations. The sales didn't go according to Martin's plan, although they sampled, no one took details or showed interest in having a dinner party with him as the chef. It was disappointing and the idea of painstakingly cooking sample food and sitting in the sun at markets was not in his vision. The following day we chatted, and I asked him if he was proud of the food he had created, which he was. The flea market wasn't part of his original plan and he was determined to make it work his way, so he wouldn't be returning. The more he spoke to people, however, the more they wanted a variation of food that was more traditional. The biggest request of this was from event's organisers, some who were friends and knew his unique flair.

Months passed, money started to dwindle and eventually Martin was backed into a financial corner and did what was expected of him. He started to create mainstream menus, and the organisers were more than happy to begin offering his services as a home chef. The food wasn't born from passion and whether Martin believed it or not, we are always steered towards our passion and life purpose, so not one booking was made - his unique artistic flair had been lost to the trap of market research, customer need analysis and the rigid business plan. The money ran out and he lost faith in himself and his dreams, heading back to corporate life, where he remains today. Sometimes I see a unique dish pop up on Facebook, but I can see that he's testing the market to check if he's creating what we want.

I still believe that had he changed his plan and his vision, by adventuring to different food and flea markets, someone would have wanted his unique chef's creations at a dinner party and his passion would be his income today. Had he not compromised his uniqueness, the rewards would have flowed in.

Very often I'm shot down for the business advice I give. I get told I don't understand the risk, because I don't have children or because I have kept my responsibilities to a minimum. Martin didn't have children or grand responsibilities either. It's not about that anyway. It's about calculated risks. The kind where you don't quit your job while you sell enough of your unique cupcakes to build up capital, or you use your savings fully aware of the risk that may or may not pay off.

In 2009, after using the money I loaned to pay off my failed business, I moved back in with my mother. My father passed away the year before and my mom had never lived by herself, so the timing was perfect. I downscaled my life to minimal expenses and let go of my vision board, which was plastered with homes, new cars and travel plans. Let's not forget that a big part of the law of attraction is setting timelines for yourself. In that version of manifestation, I was supposed to have had my own home by then. My businesses were not supposed to have failed and clinging to the business plan only pushed me further away from what my vision was supposed to look like. I empathised with Martin, because I had done it all before, but I wanted him to have enough belief in himself to take some calculated risks. He never did, but I am still determined to host a dinner party of his, with his unique flair, before he shifted his focus away from his purpose and forgot his self-worth. Martin's story isn't the only story I have of a failed attempt at entrepreneurship. I have more stories of failure than of success, and I have no intention of selling you yet another book on feel-good dreams and isolated cases of a business that started in the garage and was sold for millions. Fighting against all the odds and not giving up when the chips are down will have you questioning your purpose to degrees beyond your imagination and at that point one question will be the game changer. "Does this decision make me happy?" Yes, it's all going to weigh on the happiness factor, which once again, the banks aren't going to take seriously.

If the law of attraction works exactly the way the most basic definition of them explains, then thought should attract what you think about. Simple enough. However, we can't truly believe that feeling miserable inside but having happy thoughts to numb out the real thoughts, is going to attract abundance? We have a more complex existence than simply being able to trick ourselves into believing unhappiness can be buried under a pile of positive affirmation and pretty pictures in our imagination. We are meant to live our happiest life, but until you know what it means to be happy, how do you know how to get there?

Before doing this next exercise, move any technology that you have out of your reach. Don't be tempted to search for this answer online. Ready? Now, define happiness. Write whatever comes to mind and go beyond the textbook definition of what happiness is. Ask yourself, "what does happiness mean to me"? Don't get too stuck on the details of material possessions or even relationship or family dynamic, because then you're heading straight back to that limited perception of your potential. If you don't know, that's okay too. I didn't know for the longest time.

When I first began focusing on happiness, it was one of the hardest things I had to do, because I was so used to focusing on everyone else's that I was clueless about what it meant for me. Loving someone else wasn't my happiness, keeping the family business alive wasn't it

either. Wide open spaces were though, but that meant moving out of the city and into a smaller town lifestyle, which I still dream of today. I'm sharing one of my un-manifested visions for myself because if I wait to write this book when I only have fulfilled stories to tell, I would never get there.

I have dreamed of leaving the big city, despite the entrepreneurial success I strive for. Waking up to mountains and a view of the sky from every direction is my happiest vision for myself. Yet, I am in a country where technology hinders the ease of communicating with clients, so I can't pack up and head far away. My family dynamic doesn't provide that ease either and neither does my financial situation. However, I've made the smallest moves to head in the direction of my happiness. I live in a third floor apartment in the buzzing city, where I have a view of the trees and rooftops. I could pretend that it's ideal and fake my happiness, but my soul knows too well that I'm yearning for me, so I sit on my patio and stare at the sunset, slightly blocked by a corporate building, and check in with my happiness.

There is a continuation to the happiness exercise, which is daily and requires consistency. It's easy to fall back into old habits and thought patterns, so be conscious of functioning within your evolving discovery of what happiness means to you. This is something I would journal, as a reminder for those days when it feels much easier to slip back into old ways, instead of working through life's chaos on your way to happiness.

My greatest frustration with any of the manifestation guidance I turned to, was the assumption that I knew what I wanted. It was a pointless exercise to create a vision board, because I didn't have a clear or happy vision for myself. I couldn't plot five years ahead because I didn't know what I wanted for myself or my business. I knew that I had failed at being an entrepreneur before and I was petrified to attempt it again, but I also knew that I was destined to be a successful business owner. How did I know this? Because my only focus was connecting to my emotions and feeling what would make me happy or not. Now that goes against any business advice you'll get. Everyone tells us to take the emotion out of business and I'm telling you to entrench it in your decisions. I'm not talking about financial decisions, which we'll discuss in the chapters to come. I mean, ask yourself if your business choices are making you happy.

Greg has been very clear on how he has wanted to occupy his time in business. He is a brilliant change manager, but Lifeology's uniqueness lies in the tools we use to create that change for the client. Greg can't use someone else's formula or step into a role where he knows the client won't appreciate the holistic approach to change, so he guided himself by happiness. We got to a point in the business where money had completely run out and despite being in our thirties, we were being told what to do by our parents. They looked at their children and saw suffering and despair, so Greg's parents asked him if it would not be safer to go back to full time employment. He knew that would make him even more unhappy, so the hunt for work increased and he contacted everyone he knew until an opportunity for contract work came up.

As it happens, the potential client wanted their own approach to corporate change. Desperate for money and holding on tight to our fraying business, Greg and I looked at the opportunity and we both agreed that he had to turn it down. Unclear on what happiness truly meant for us, we knew that we were moving away from our happiness if we didn't use the Lifeology tools we had taken so long to develop and believe in. Happiness meant moving towards our purpose and that was good enough to cling to. Not waiting until the end of the book for the happy ending. Over the next few years, Greg has had corporate change management clients who have welcomed our holistic approach and his happiness is still his guide as he embarks on the decision to accept or decline the next contract.

Setting my compass to happiness is a visualisation I have done for almost six years. Before then, my ego was having a field day deciding what happiness should look like. It was an illusion, masked in safety, with hardly any reason to test my degree of bravery or stretch myself into the depth of my purpose.

This visualisation is one that can be done anywhere where you can close your eyes for a while - in the shower, floating in the pool, on your Uber ride - as long as you try do it at least three times a week. This is like exercise. The more you commit to attracting happiness, the greater chance you have of sculpting the happiness you want. Painting the illusion of happiness is fool's play, so get comfortable and let a few breaths relax you.

Now, imagine you see a compass in your hand, and you look East first. Move clockwise to South, then West and when you look at what should be North, it says "HAPPINESS". Imagine yourself on your path to happiness and don't try figure out where it will take you. Just as you would follow true North, follow your Happiness to where it wants to guide you. This visualisation is about activating the feeling of happiness. Focus on the compass and what it feels like to confidently walk in the direction of your happiness.

Even if your life seems to be in absolute chaos at the moment, give yourself the gentle reminder of what happiness feels like. I've heard it all before, so if you

believe you've never felt happiness a day in your life, you should do this exercise daily and give yourself permission to drop the obstacles and feel at least a glimmer of imagined happiness. This exercise of setting your compass to happiness will steer you in the right direction, no matter how unsure you are of where you want to be or what you will be like when you are happy. The worst case scenario, if you can't begin to imagine happiness, is to say it a few times in your head while you imagine your compass taking you there. It's not uncommon and not a bad thing either. It's simply more of an adventure to discover where you're heading to.

Some days I only need to imagine walking for a few minutes and on other days I do the visualisation until it calms me, and I can finally fall asleep. Remember not to try figure out where your happiness path is taking you, but trust that each day's opportunities and choices will help you get there. This visualisation is only one step, so don't feel lost in the process of the aimless wondering. Enjoy it, because the adventures are underway.

Chances are you'll find happiness in the most unexpected business places, like I did. When Lifeology hadn't made any money in the first quarter, Greg and I decided to change our marketing angle again, although we had no idea what that new angle would be. It was December 2009 and not much time for action, while businesses rested for the festive season, we took ourselves to the movies instead. We watched Julie and Julia, a story about a daily blogger and how it changed her life. I had been playing around on Twitter at that stage and although by South African perception I was wasting my time, I had built up a decent following and was watching how the Americans and British used the social network. Blogging was growing in popularity, so it seemed like the natural marketing progression to begin sharing our Lifeology teachings in order to gain the attention of potential clients. I was single, obsessed with my weight and struggling to earn a living, which made me the ideal target market for my own business services. It's the typical story of the ballet teacher, who never becomes the ballerina. I wanted to be the ballerina, so I started my blog, Project Me, on 1 January 2010.

I committed to blogging daily, for a year and started to share my stories of day to day living, my slogan, which was ...totally goalless yet absolutely purposeful! We kept to the by-line of courage, consciousness and a sense of humour, and my Twitter and blog following grew. My Facebook friends began to engage and support me. While Greg and I struggled through each day of trying to figure out why the clients weren't coming, I kept Project Me real and shared all the levels of entrepreneurial despair, as well as the determination to keep on going until I made money from my purpose. Sharing my journey of self-discovery made it clearer that I was on the right path and nothing besides teaching would fulfil me.

While Greg worked on finding clients who would use our formula for bringing about change to their business or lives, I worked on turning "manifestation myths" into a product people needed. We had the odd night class going, but it was neither change management nor manifestation based. It was still the metaphysics work we were teaching, and it was frustrating us both. I focused tirelessly on using social media to gain the attention of potential clients and kept it authentic in my views of manifestation and happiness. While my Twitter following grew to tens of thousands, our funds dwindled by the same amount. Desperation set in and we convinced ourselves that it was because we thought out the box and should have stuck to what the business books were saying, so we tried that too. After the first few cold calls, we both knew we were terribly off course and quickly made happiness our priority again.

At that point, a friend got hold of me and said he had given my name to the Joburg Theatre, to blog about an upcoming show. I didn't do that. My blog wasn't lifestyle or entertainment. My blog was self-help and that wasn't helpful at all. After some convincing, I embraced the challenge and blogged my first entertainment piece. The change was petrifying, with fears of people losing interest and me steering myself off course from my vision of workshops, talks and seminars on manifestation. But we don't only have one passion, and over the months, social networking allowed me to see how much I enjoyed networking. I began using my Twitter following to connect South Africans with what they needed and called it, #FollowSA. This had helped my public visibility, which I wanted to use to grow Lifeology in the direction we always intended. At the time, being pushed to do an entertainment blog post had felt like a mere distraction instead of a shift in direction along my path to happiness.

It didn't take long, however, for me to fall in love with the theatre and I became a regular blogger, who never missed a show. Still purpose driven, I found a lesson in every theatre production I watched and managed to keep the theme very #ProjectMe. Everyone loved it and my following grew even more. My bank account didn't, however. Once again, I felt off course and wanted to give up the blogging and focus even more on making the business plan and service offering work. I didn't have the realisation first, to be honest. I got to the desperate space and only took in the lesson after, but eventually I was forced to say yes to something completely different.

After yet another year of no substantial income, the capital ran out and we were on loaned money. It was time to think outside the box or give up on the dream, so I focused more on my newfound passion for social media and looked at how I could make money through that medium. #FollowSA had turned into successful social networking events, and Lifeology was gaining exposure and opportunities to travel across South Africa and host meet -ups. We were hosting over a hundred people at venues who were sponsoring everything except the drinks and Lifeology was finally keeping me busy and heading towards making an income.

The plan was simple. We would simply add on an entrance fee and small amount for brands to continue to be involved, because both the brands and the online community were gaining so much from the events. For minimal work, some brands were receiving over a hundred online mentions in a night. However, the second we added the fee, everything dried up. No one came to the meet-ups, despite the price being equivalent to one drink. It didn't matter though, because the prizes and offers of sponsorship vanished too. We said goodbye to our well thought-out plan and were back to square one.

The one thing I had gained though, was an amazing network of people and great exposure for my personal brand. Unfortunately, that wasn't helping though, and no matter how hard I tried to keep pushing myself back to the original business model, something wasn't allowing the flow of success. I can't count the number of brainstorms Greg and I had and the countless times we tried to figure out what we were getting wrong. All I wanted to do was teach and write. I also wanted to carry on having the fun I had discovered social networking to be, but it was 2010 and no one was making money from social networking then, so it was give up the dream or surrender to whatever would help us keep that dream alive. If we had given up, we wouldn't have deserved to have Lifeology anyway. The whole foundation of the business is about having the courage to carry on.

That decision shifted everything and at the end of 2010 I was called to a meeting at the Joburg Theatre where they asked me if I would take over the social media and do online publicity for three of the upcoming shows. It was a temporary offer. It was also something I had never done before. 'Social Media Publicist' wasn't even a recognised job title yet. The true courage weighed on putting down the original business plan and deciding if the opportunity still fed my passion and would make me happy. I was petrified, but when I reassessed my dreams, the potential was still alive. It was a consultancy offer, with our first retainer business and still allowed for us to pursue our vision for Lifeology. The story will continue to unfold, but that was the start of our opportunity to begin our second business, Chat Factory Online Social Media Agency. I didn't know it then, but I was ticking boxes that fulfilled my purpose and would help me create more of the vision I had for myself. Our business had a plan, we were just less in control of it than the textbooks lead us to believe.

I'm currently working with Jim, who had two failed businesses and is studying his MBA in the hopes that it will give him a clearer idea of what type of business he should have. He is determined to be an entrepreneur, but he's hunting for what he thinks the market requires of him. The reason is because Jim has no idea what his purpose or his passion is. He admits that the MBA isn't helping him uncover that, because all he knows are his failures. If you've come this far and you're still unsure of what your future looks like or what will make you happy, you're not alone. Like where I began, if you are doing what you love but the success hasn't come and it's tempting to give up, hang on a little while longer. Sadly, not every story ends in success, but we've got a good shot at if we shift our focus in an unchartered direction.

I'm going to straight up blame the misguided hopes people place on vision boards and ask you to collect any that you've already done. You don't have to destroy them, although you may want to in a few months. For now, look at each picture or word you selected and ask yourself, "what's my purpose behind my choice?" If it feels as though it will truly fulfil you, then it can stay. Watch for the trap of limitations though. Have you placed actual figures or exact car models? If that motivates you, then make sure you have a very strong

reminder that this vision board is a mere stepping-stone to the next one. Trust me, when your income exceeds amounts you can only imagine, you will know you can achieve more.

The moral of the story is to give yourself permission to change your mind. It may sound simple, yet change is the root of most fear. The more you are afraid, the more you get in your own way and the less chance you'll have of seeing your plans turn into success stories. The law of attraction is right there waiting to be used correctly and the game changer is to focus on how you feel about what you want to manifest and not the image of the dream. We are pure energy. That's science 101 and believe it not, knowing that is vital for the success of your business. You don't have to see the sun for it to burn warm on your skin and you don't have to see your dreams either, but you do have to feel them. For that potential client to be manifested into reality, you have to feel the gratitude before they even find you. Can you imagine the feeling of when you hold the keys to your first office space or sign your largest client on?

Although I'm telling you to unlearn what you have about manifestation, it's time to rebuild trust in the law of attraction by creating your ever-evolving business plan.

Can you think of an achievement that you will always be proud of? When I was six years old my mother entered me into a beauty pageant for the local newspaper and my picture was in it. I remember the day of the photographs so clearly and I felt like a princess. With all the eagerness of a winner, I waited to win, but that never materialised. I was bitterly disappointed and decided I wasn't pretty. When the opportunity came to enter a dress -up competition at the local movie house, I was gently nudged by my mother and went along with my sisters, who were eager to win and confidently dressed up. As little as I was, I think I got some element of manifestation because I wanted to go as Miss Universe and feel like the winner of that first pageant. My mother did my hair and makeup like she had for the photo shoot before, and I tentatively took to the stage, with butterflies in my tummy and nasty words of failure in my head. I won the competition that day and I still rely on that memory to push me to get back up when I fall down. That was a notable achievement at an early age, but most people would focus on having not won the more glamourous pageant. We do it to ourselves on a daily basis, by focusing on what we have to improve about ourselves, instead of the achievements, no matter how small they may seem. Focusing on your achievements will, in fact, be the catalyst for manifest more of what you want.

You are powerful, but you're not that powerful! Meaning, you have limitless potential to manifest what you want, but you can't determine the course life will take you on to get there. That's where most people get tripped up, starting with placing timeframes when you want the universe to deliver your dream. Go ahead and set timeframes for yourself, but not for your manifestations. You also don't have the power to determine what your reality will look like, because you will always limit yourself to what you believe you can achieve. If you ask for two clients and a third one manifests, are you going to turn them down? I don't think so. What you should be focusing on is knowing you can manifest all the clients you need and then the ball is back in your court. For every ideal you have in your business plan, you should have five actions to manifest it into reality.

Try it, now. In your journal, write down at least two ideals that will make up your business plan. Be it new clients, more media exposure, your social media video going viral, or one big sale of your products or services. If you have a financial target you have to meet, put that down too. Now, for each point, list five actions that you need to actively take in order to manifest your business plan into reality. Those actions need to go into your

diary as tasks for specific days. No matter how much it scares you or how busy your days become, putting that task off, but expecting the universe to deliver isn't fair on you or the demands you place on the universe. At this point, or when your business plan becomes clearer, make sure you design your vision for your business with the demands on you and not your dreams.

Hard work aside, the amount of time you spend not taking action is as vital. In that time, you're going to be still and imagine your plans into reality. I can't stress enough how important it is to feel your business into fruition. My least favourite question is, "where do you see yourself in five years?" but now I'm going to ask it of you, with one change to the question. I want to know, "where do you see yourself when you are abundantly happy?" Who wants to wait five years anyway?

This visualisation should be done at least once a week and may cause some initial frustration, especially if you feel way off course, but the sooner you begin, the better. It's like medicine for the wounded esteem. If you aren't disciplined or the process unsettles you, then put the allocated times in your diary for the next six months. If you use an alarm clock on your phone, even better, set the alert to wake you five minutes earlier, once a week and get manifesting.

Find time to be comfortable and quiet for a while, where you won't be disturbed as you plot your path to success. Your mind is going to be active in this process and so are your emotions. Imagine a day in your life when you have achieved all you could wish for, with a healed version of yourself. Start from the moment you wake up and imagine the feeling of opening your eyes in

your dream home, with your full day waiting for you. It's brimming with opportunities and as you imagine your way through a specific board meeting or arriving at the airport for an international flight, focus on the feelings of self-pride, excitement, achievement and determination.

Don't stress if you have no clue what your day will look like because the more you do this process, the clearer it will become. It can also change at any time. When I began my imagining, I had huge office in the buzzing city, but I slowly realised that I have anchored myself close to my family because I'm a natural caretaker. One day my family dynamic will change, and I will be stuck in the city, so I started to change my plans for myself and imagine wide open space and the feeling of stepping outside in the morning and breathing in the fresh country air. Of course, my business plans had to change to suit to my desire to be out of the city and now I imagine a dynamic team working closely with the clients so I can come back to the city a few times a month. I'm not there yet, but I do have my third-floor apartment, overlooking the treetops and giving me the feeling of slightly wider, more open spaces. You can also shift and mould your plans as you figure yourself out. It's actually the most fun you can have with your plans and on the day, you turn a vision into reality, you'll never want to stop turning your imagination into your reality.

In the final step of this action-packed chapter, let's change the game and revamp your vision board to a powerful map to manifestation, which I call the "Achievement Board".

You're going to need a pin board or a surface where you can constantly add and move pictures around. You're also going to need ribbon or string, to divide the board into quarters. Put your empty board up and choose one of the quarters to be your vision corner. Now that you have a clearer understanding of manifesting without time and limitation, go ahead and put up material or reachable goals. Remember that you don't have control of the timeframe of manifestation, but you do have control of the actions you can take to bring the manifestation to reality.

I had a designer handbag pinned in my visualisation corner for years. I grew up in a bargain-hunting family, who would remark on how expensive everything was, even if it was dirt-cheap. It made me count pennies as I grew up, but worse, I never desired the ownership of anything materially beautiful. I was stuck in necessity, but slowly realised I deserved more, and I started with a handbag. No more rip-offs for me. It took me years, but it also took me to a new level of desire to manifest. I knew if I could earn enough in my business to buy that handbag, then I could reach higher.

Time passed and my dream began to dwindle because seasons of fashion change and after one summer sale, I knew it would be gone. So, I saved up what I could and kept the vision real, imagining the elated joy I would have when I paid for it. Two seasons passed, our first retainer client was paying Lifeology and things were looking up, so we went shopping. I still well up with emotion when I think about the moment, I saw that very handbag in the luggage shop window. My vision board was on display for the world to see, so my

business partner knew it well and he gave me a reassuring nod, that it was time to buy the bag. I don't think the shop assistants will forget the moment I hugged the handbag and said, "thank you Universe". When I got home, I moved the picture of the handbag from my vision corner to the achievement side of the board.

When it comes to finance, do the same thing. I had a clear amount in my head of what I wanted my business to bring in for the month. One month was good enough, just to know we could do it and when we did, I moved the picture I had created to resemble the amount and placed it on the achievement side. I then upped the stakes and have the next vision of financial abundance to achieve.

My achievement board is ever growing, with photographs from trips overseas and printed out compliments from clients. It's brimming with feelings of success and has become the fuel to drive me forward as my Highest Esteem craves even more with each achievement.

You get the picture, right?

We manifest from positive and while the world places false hope on a motivational meme, you're fuelling your life with testaments of your ability to achieve anything. You are turning yourself into your own positive affirmation. You are tossing out quotes from ancient gurus and writing your own manifestation mantra. You are learning that you are smart and brave enough to achieve anything because you've done it before. One small milestone at a time.

American mythologist Joseph Campbell said, "We have to let go of the life we have planned, to accept the one that is waiting for us."

4

PROCRASTINATION VS. ACHIEVING

I am a great procrastinator. It took me nearly five years to finally settle down and write this book and an additional year to get to this point, after finding my publishing partner. I can't say there was a day that went by when I didn't want to bring this dream to a reality. I also can't say I consciously set out to sabotage my dreams.

Instead of empathising with ourselves when procrastination kicks in, we bash the self-esteem around further, not uncovering the reasons why we are avoiding the work that needs to be done. Essentially, all we are doing is delaying actions which will get us closer to our success, yet there's no motivation to buckle down and tackle the task. Procrastinating isn't something to be brushed off and swept under a pile of motivational quotes. In fact, those are potentially destructive in a time when fear is holding you back and you haven't uncovered the hidden potential waiting for you.

When our plans overwhelm us and cause procrastination, there is always a reason. Fear has been downplayed to something that isn't real and can easily be overcome by standing in front of a mirror and chanting a few affirmations. But when you're in the midst of a low self-esteem attack and haven't established your foundation of self-worth, no amount of demanding your fears away is going to work. Chances are, it will only perpetuate it more and focusing on affirming positivity could be that procrastination tactic you begin to rely on.

We all have that Facebook friend who is going nowhere slowly, but spends hours posting positive quotes and articles on the steps to overcome fears and procrastination. Yes, that friend. If you're that person, allow yourself to learn from the reasons why you can't simply snap your fingers and get rid of the avoidances. There are a few reasons why. If you are at the beginning of your entrepreneurial ventures and you feel as though you know what makes you happy and have worked through the first few chapters, but still feel lost along the path, then it's time to uncover the fears which are holding you back.

In this journal exercise, take a look at each of the potential reasons why you could be procrastinating and write an empathetic sentence about the reasons you relate to the procrastination:

- ***Fear of the outcome***
- ***Feeling under-resourced***
- ***Overwhelmed by the amount of work that lies ahead***
- ***No idea where to begin***
- ***You're a perfectionist and it has to be right the first time***
- ***Laziness***
- ***Rebellion***
- ***Your plan doesn't feel like your true purpose***
- ***Lack of motivation***
- ***Fatigue***
- ***You're not having fun***
- ***Boredom when tackling tasks***

- ***Fear of failure***

I could relate to at least five of these at any one time, but the key to making fears magically disappear is not in chanting them away, but in meeting them halfway. My longest time of procrastination is at the beginning, because I don't work in a methodical order at the best of times and I have no idea where to start on a new project.

My procrastination tactic can become obsessing on the initial step in the process and never getting any further, but that's because I also have a fear of failure and used to be stuck on getting it right the first time. If business teaches you anything, it's that getting it right is only mastered by trial and error. The error part had the potential to cripple me, which stems from my family dynamic of each sibling trying to outshine the other.

That is an inherent trait; because my parents were always in competition and if my mother made soup on Monday, my father would try outsmarting her on Tuesday. Sitting at the dinner table after school was a fierce competition about who could get the most attention from a family of seven. That still lingers in my family today, yet I have learned to focus on my own achievements and only concern myself with my own praise and recognition. It may sound harsh, but even turning my attention to obsessing over fixing the family dynamic became a brilliant way to procrastinate.

Deeper in the chapter we are going to tackle the reasons why you procrastinate, but consciousness precedes success, and understanding your

procrastination tactics will give you great insight moving forward. Keep your journal with you over the next few days and keep a few pages blank to keep notes of what you learn about your procrastination.

- ***When do you procrastinate the most?***
- ***What triggers your procrastination?***
- ***How long do you procrastinate for?***
- ***What kicks you back into action?***

How long can you stay focused on the task before searching for an avoidance tactic again?

How do you feel when you acknowledge your avoidance of what needs to be done?

Shining light on the parts of your personality, which have been hiding in the shadows is incredibly powerful! Merely taking the time to understand your procrastination shows great self-empathy and will ease your esteem into greater moments of bravery. You don't need to do much more than watch your patterns and acknowledge your patterns in this exercise.

With an adjustment of attitude towards your stagnant moments in the process of developing your business, you will begin to see the procrastination times which require internal assessment. It seems so easy to imagine the limitless possibilities of entrepreneurship, but getting stuck right at the beginning is a reality. If it's not happening there, then the first hiccup or failed plan can throw the esteem off and put on the breaks. Your business will always work in cycles and halting fears will continuously emerge. Procrastination isn't going anywhere, but it can become a guardian from the very beginning.

My consciousness preceded my success because I took the time to figure out what got me stuck right at the beginning of my third business. With two failed businesses lagging behind in everything I did, I became obsessed with making perfect decisions for my new business. While I was doing that, Greg was new to entrepreneurship and had his own obsessions. Yet, all we should have done was head in the direction where practicality and passion meet. In the chapters before, we uncovered internal strengths and set the direction for happiness, but that doesn't give you a practical foundation for your business. Whether you are getting started or have a solid business direction, paving your way forward requires a fortune of business-mindedness.

Far too many people have said to me they know they are supposed to be an entrepreneur, but that is not a good enough motivation for success. Neither is having that passion without utilising your business strengths. Once I discovered my passion for writing, I knew that was all I wanted to do. The whole business plan for Lifeology was built around my passion and ability to write. I was doing amazingly as a writer and my audience grew, but my business didn't. The frustration was immense, because I was doing what I loved, moving towards my happiness and visualising it on a daily basis. Yet, where was the money? Where were the clients? I would sit on the couch and cry, mumbling to myself, "I just want to write". That hasn't changed. To this day, all I want to do is write. It's my greatest passion because I've learned that it's the strongest tool to teaching, which feeds my purpose. Unfortunately, business is way more practical than that and you may be stuck at the starting line, asking yourself what your business offering should even look like.

Doing what you are good at is not necessarily what you should be offering the world, as I discovered in the beauty industry. Doing what you love may not be what can keep your business sustainable, which I uncovered when I thought #FollowSA was the answer to my financial woes. Don't ignore this step because your business is already in motion. These questions have the ability to move you to the next phase, no matter how far along you may feel you are. Through the constant returning to some of these, we went from imagining owning one business to successfully having two. We stopped throwing money at marketing consultants because it's now a skill I never knew I had. It's unstudied, but I developed it by taking the time to watch what I was naturally good at. Don't assume that your natural talents are going to be your business offering when they could be the catalyst to your business skills. Not every person who can bake a cake that their friends would pay for is destined to be the next Cake Boss.

My favourite thing to do is watch people's faces when I respond to their question of my background to my social media company and I tell them I studied secretarial and beauty therapy.

These questions hold the very joy of what it means to be an entrepreneur. If you wanted to work within the confines of your studies and what you know you are good at, then you could have kept your day job, but you don't want that, do you?

I suggest you do this exercise on your laptop because it can be fleshed out into a working plan from there. It's time to focus on your skills and service offering, while bringing these aspects of yourself into the light. Ask yourself these practical questions, one at a time. Don't move onto the next one until the first is answered because you want all elements of esteem to move through the point you are focusing on. Write down as much as you can about each one.

- ***Is what you studied or mastered your way of making money?***

- ***What is your skillset, and did you enjoy developing it?***
- ***Did you learn skills along the way that you would like to incorporate into your***
- ***business?***
- ***What are you naturally good at?***
- ***What aspects of entrepreneurship excite you?***
- ***Which parts of being an entrepreneur would you prefer not to deal with?***
- ***How confident are you in dealing with the business side of entrepreneurship?***
- ***How much time and capital do you have to support this current phase of your business?***

Like physical exercise, only repetition is going to make you strong. One whirl at these questions could give you a burst of energy to fuel a few days of enthusiasm, but that will soon fade, and you'll go back to your natural routine of procrastinating. Whether you're going into business with a partner or venturing out on your own, include these into your monthly meetings. Yep, even if you're flying solo, have at least one check-in with yourself a month because it's the fuel which will keep you on track and help put deadlines in place.

If you're going back to things you should have done months ago and can't seem to get yourself moving, then you have to ask yourself why the desire for entrepreneurship isn't enough to fuel your motivation?

Okay, gloves off! The reality is, entrepreneurs are fighting to improve their services and figure out what they can do to bring in the bucks, but the hardest parts of entrepreneurship is holding on while you discover what you can endure. No matter how many safety nets you think are in place or business courses you do in preparation, nothing prepares you for the emotional challenges which lie ahead. I've read my fair share of business books, which all seem to skip over the shameful parts of the climb to the top. No one wants to be seen as vulnerable in the business space, bearing the truth about the overwhelming fears and moments of despair. Even the great stories of success fail to focus on the parts where quitting is the only thing that seems real at one point in time. Yes, they make it in the end, but emotional milestones need to be used as the stepping-stones to success and that can't be glazed over.

How much help do you think successful entrepreneurs have received along the way? Whatever you imagine it may be, you should multiply it by a few hundred. Asking for help and showing vulnerability is believed to be shameful. There is a myth that overcoming business challenges on your own builds character or makes for better entrepreneurship, but the opposite has proven to be true too.

Debt is easy to accumulate in a business and when suppliers build a relationship on trust, they allow you take the products or the service and pay later. Eventually later comes and you've done that with more than one service provider, so there are mountains of bills outstanding. My ex business partner and I found ourselves in that position within the first few years of our business, and by 2005 we were drowning in bills. It was easy to get credit then and whenever we could take loans, we did. Coming from the family dynamic of 'everyone knows best', the last thing I intended to do was show my vulnerability and ask for help of any kind. We needed it, but had so many plans to get out of debt before it got too much to handle. The less we managed to do that, however, the more shame crept in. The banks started to want payments and threatened to take our assets. Month end was a nightmare, fearing each phone call and SMS we would receive. They were all demanding money and turning to anyone by that time was far too late. How do you admit such poor business handling, even if it came from a place of fear and shame?

In 2008 we did the unthinkable and went to a cousin of a cousin who owned one of those betting bars. He was willing to loan us the money, at nearly double the interest rate, but also assured us of time to pay it off. We cleared the debt with the bank and suppliers, but soon discovered the dangerous world we stepped into. You don't have paper trails of this kind of loan, so when it gets called in, there's no one to defend you. When I think back now, I always wonder if I had any clue how smart I was then, because I sure took the dumb path. In no time, the inevitable happened and I was forced to turn to my mother, while my business partner had to tell her siblings. We both dipped into money from our inheritances, which teaches unexplainable lessons about asking for help as soon as you need it.

There are three times in business where it's impossible to make it impersonal - when faced with a critical choice, uncomfortable change or unexpected chaos. The advice that filters through every message to an entrepreneur is to take the emotion out of all your decisions, but how does one do that when you feel as though you birthed your business? It takes that kind of nurturing in the beginning, or at least, it should. Depending on the personality type and degree of attachment, it can be a highly emotional experience to go through any phase of a business. Not having permission to honour your emotions of fear and deal with the shame that engulfs any failed milestone, is a flaw in your business plan. This isn't a harsh statement to add criticism to an already overwhelming process. It's empathetic encouragement for you to fill your business with all the emotions that have been bottled up while you've been trying to make adult choices as an entrepreneur. If you aren't feeling overwhelmed by the process and manage to push past the procrastination, then high five yourself. If not, now is a good time to master the art of bringing the right amount of emotion in to deal with the change, choices and unforeseeable chaos.

It's nearly impossible to argue with science, even when it takes away the copouts we comfortably rely on. I'm talking about fear. I'm also talking about excitement. The proven fact is that the body's reaction to them is exactly the same; it's only the mind that decides the difference. The butterflies in your stomach are awful when the brain signals fear, but overwhelmingly thrilling when it's sensed as fun. Jumping out of an airplane sounds like the worst idea imaginable to me, but tell me I can stand in front of a few thousand people and speak, then the adrenalin of pure joy flows through me. If I said, do one thing each day that thrills you, you could probably make a list for days.

Now if I say, do one thing each day which scares you, feelings of anxiety and distress should already be seeping through. That's purely because you've decided it should feel that way. I'm not saying it's easy, but it's possible to turn the things that scare you into the moments that thrill you. This was a real turning point in business for Greg and me. We still practice this today; despite many people thinking we take our business on with fierce bravery and boldness. Behind closed doors, each time we get together, we thrash out what is holding us back and promise ourselves that we will do one or two things each day that scares us.

The Universe rewards bravery. That's less scientifically proven, but proving it to yourself will slowly build your business into something greater than you ever expected. Fears are irrational. We get told that all the time, but it doesn't make them easier to overcome. Fears also stem from some part of our past, known or unknown to us. I happen to remember one of my triggers to fear and although it may seem totally absurd to others, it was holding me back in business. When I was about seven years old, way before cell phones, my dad left me in a restaurant accidentally. He told me to go to the bathroom and wait for him, while he slipped into the men's room. My mother knew he had me, so everyone piled into the car. He forgot me and drove off, while I strolled back into the entrance and waited inside as I had been told. For a little girl, it felt like forever before someone noticed I had been left behind. I remember the bowl of mints the manager put in front of me. It was before our days of hygiene neurosis and I sifted through them to find the pastel pink ones. My dad would never leave me. How could my whole family forget me? But they did and he had.

My family giggles at the story today, but in the hour or so I waited for my family to notice that I was missing and come back to fetch me, the incident had scarred me for life. To this day, I'm petrified of being lost and forgotten, with no one ever knowing I'm missing. It's caused an irrational fear of elevators, resulting in my inability to go in one on my own, in case it gets stuck and I'm there for hours on end, never to be found. It also causes terrible distress when I have to travel on my own, so I don't. That's not ideal for an entrepreneur who is trying to make her way in the world. I actually have to go into the world to do that, which I managed to avoid for years. In the beginning of our business days it was easy - Greg and I attended every meeting together. I didn't have to panic about getting lost or going up tall buildings by myself. Then the unthinkable happened. Our business grew. Greg went off to his clients and I had to go off to mine. Before the days of GPS on our cell phones, he plotted out directions on maps for me and I cried for hours before heading on my way. How irrational does this all sound? Yes, I know, but that's what fear does to us. To this day, I implement the 'one thing that scares me' rule, when I adventure to a new client or unknown place. I've made it easier for myself by relying on the GPS and have even asked a security guard to travel up the elevator with me, or faked searching in my bag for something until someone else comes along and used the elevator at the same time.

I'm telling you this, because your fears could be way more complicated or rational than mine, but unless you first overcome the shame and find empathy for yourself, you are never going to ask for help or take steps to change things - and so you will procrastinate. There are thousands of people who want to be entrepreneurs and there is nothing new under the sun, so if you don't move fast, someone is going to beat you to it. We don't want that!

Overcoming procrastination and tackling fears simultaneously takes some practical planning. It's a methodical process with two different areas of focus and an exercise which should become part of your daily business practice from this day on. As an entrepreneur, there's no getting away from an electronic device or good old-fashioned paper diary. If that's not a practice already, change that now.

Dropping the ball is a reality if you don't have your appointments and to-do list. Any article that says you should be efficient or passionate enough to work without one, is leading you to a fool's paradise. We are not machines and we aren't meant to remember everything we have to do at all times, nor are we capable of doing everything in the moment. The reason is a simple one. Life happens. You can plan in your head all you like, but you can't prepare for the curveballs that fill your day, and remember - everything is not a challenge you should strive to master.

Instead, end your day with your diary and make notes of what you didn't get done by carrying it over to the next opportune moment. Don't push it out too far, because that's procrastination. Make sure all your appointments are in the diary and then reflect on your day and see if you did the one thing that scares you. If you didn't manage to, move it to the next day, remembering that carrying it over too long is perpetuating fear and is holding back something exciting for your business.

It may be as scary and simple as responding to an email, making a phone call, confronting a client or looking at an outstanding bill to be paid. If you did it,

be mighty proud of yourself and decide on the next thing you will do the following day. Overcoming fears is an accomplishment of its own, so add them to your achievement board and celebrate them. This is still a daily practice of mine and I'm so grateful for it. Some days it is a client email I don't want to face, and other days it's accepting a thrilling opportunity I've been dreaming up for years.

Once that is done, take a moment to imagine the thing that scares you and feel the fear in your body. Simply be still and feel it. Does it make your heart race, palms sweaty, tummy churn? Now imagine that same feeling in something you love, be it planning a weekend away or your adrenalin rush. Train your brain to feel the fear less and thrive on the excitement of your business as much as your adventures, and you will feel the fear become less daunting. Amazingly, being brave enough to start this daily practice will be the first challenge, so write it in your diary for tomorrow.

I repeat, the Universe rewards bravery!

5

FEAR VS. F.A.I.T.H

We underestimate the amount of consciousness and work it takes to function from faith. Like love, each person has their unique understanding and expression of faith, but also like love, we have all been let down by it. The traditional definitions directly link it to religion first. Further down the list of possible meanings, the Cambridge English Dictionary states, "faith: great trust or confidence in something or someone." I like that definition. It may seem out of context to make faith part of your best business practice, but when that trust and confidence is found within, and the something or someone you rely on is yourself, it becomes the strongest business tool you have.

My discovery of faith didn't begin in the business world. It began like many others, in someone else's story. Some find those stories in the written word, or myths or living examples, but I discovered mine in death. My walk through life has led me to every religion and belief system imaginable. They call people like me 'seekers' because we are always wanderers of the world, seeking the truth and losing faith in it as soon as we discover it. After my business burned down, I lost my faith and began a new path of wandering, where I found Shamanic healing. It was a fascinating time in my life and my spiritual teacher imparted so much knowledge, which I thought would be a path I would follow forever.

In the circle of students was an incredibly spiritual woman, who made meditation cushions and many other hand crafts for a living. Her hair was long, which fitted the shamanic theme of the circle and in my late twenties, my newfound friends helped make everything right in my world. Then one day the craft woman got sick. She had a debilitating headache and although I wasn't at the healing circle, they had one for her. When word got to me, my intuition yelled out to get her to a hospital, but the students I was with told me they were all in a great state of faith that she would be well soon.

But she didn't get well soon. She died. She had meningitis and no amount of faith would have saved her. I immediately lost faith in that circle of people. Not in Shamanism, because it is still very close to my heart, but I certainly couldn't comprehend the faith they had relied on to overlook the need for modern medicine.

The seeker in me fell into deep turmoil after that and I returned to the aimless searching. I was determined to understand faith from the perspective of taking responsibility and action. Although my obsession with faith was supposed to be practiced in my personal life, I was at a crucial stage in Lifeology, where I was feeling my faith wavering the most. Imagine having truly found your passion and a way to turn it into a viable business. Now imagine being broke on that dream. Isn't that the exact opposite of what the law of attraction teaches us? I was determined and positive, while ticking all the boxes of a passionate, determined entrepreneur, but the clients weren't coming. With each passing day of giving everything to my business, the faith in myself and my dreams began to waiver. It got to the point where we were absolutely broke. I was living off my mother, Greg and I were loaning money wherever we could because, as a rule, banks don't give loans or overdrafts to budding entrepreneurs. I was caught between despairing fear and spiritual confusion, feeling that my very beliefs had failed me.

Restoring faith is needed along our path to success as much as it is in any other part of life. Business faith is not passive, and it's not filled with hope and positive vibes. It is a conscious, focused part of your daily routine.

Contrary to the over-simplification of manifestation, being positive and passionate is not enough. By now you should have a clearer understanding of the destruction caused by denying your truth and painting your reality with false happiness. The same applies with holding onto faith when it comes from a place of fear.

You cannot function in faith and fear at the same time.

As with positive affirmations, if faith comes from a place of desperation, the chances of it manifesting into success stories is a miracle in itself. I'm all for bringing the esoteric manifestations into the boardroom but holding out for a miracle isn't something I have relied on. Instead, I worked fiercely at becoming still and meditating on what faith looked like in the business world. The meditation only took a few minutes though, and the rest of the time I was weaving instinctive elements of consciousness and action into my businesses. Eventually, I turned faith into an acronym, with each word designed to enhance my consciousness and align my plans with daily acts of faith.

The acronym and practice of business FAITH:

- ***Focus***
- ***Acceptance***
- ***Intention***
- ***Trust***
- ***Happiness***

These five elements of faith will be practiced in a breathing exercise and are more about becoming conscious than about the actions that need to be taken. We are always searching for what we can do to make things happen for us, but the essence of greatest spiritual teachings constantly tries to instil in us, that it's in the 'not doing' where manifestation happens. And 'not doing' is almost impossible for us to do in this modern world, where we feel as though we always have to hustle. This acronym of faith is asking you to stop! Stop over analysing and exhausting your mind while you try to figure out a plan and the determination to find the solutions to everything.

The hardest lesson I have had to learn is that it's perfectly normal to not have the solutions to life. It's absolutely okay to not know if the next business decision will be the right one. Feeling absolutely certain is a rare life experience and business advice, preaching crystal clear plans is mastered by few. Some of the most valuable crystals I own are flawed and full of earth's murky mysteries.

We are about to begin understanding the sequence of five breaths you will take, focusing your intention on each of these words: Focus, Acceptance, Intention, Trust and Happiness. These are not 'steps', which have become the media's hypnotic tool to provide us with the answers to anything. It's almost impossible to find an article which doesn't begin with, "The 5 steps to," or "10 actions every entrepreneur should," or "Integrate these 5 habits into your routine". They have become the quick fix drug for the desperate, which we are consciously choosing not to be.

The only steps you need to take are walking your own path, in FAITH.

This business faith isn't the replacement of any other faith you have in your life and it's not born from the essence of fundamental beliefs. It's a practical tool to be used, with the underlying purpose of calming the frightened ego and keeping you conscious and engaged through your entrepreneurial process.

. . .

Focus

When fear overwhelms the businessperson, the first aspect of discipline to fall by the wayside is focus. It becomes a mad scramble to do anything to plug the holes of failure. A little of everything becomes the game plan with the perceived hope that throwing the net wide enough will be sure to catch something. The most basic teaching of Eastern philosophy is cantered around mastering the art of discipline. It is believed that self-control is fundamental to overall wellbeing, with mindfulness having the power to create, heal and restore. Your business needs as much mindfulness as your body does, and the practice of focusing will allow you to take control of the wellbeing of yourself and your business.

Focus is not about what you do, but how you do it and it's not to be confused with the creative energy of multi- tasking. I don't have the ability to sit down and do one task from beginning to end. I feel as though my body is going to explode with curiosity about all I'm missing in the world if I work on one task for too long. A few months ago, I read an article saying entrepreneurs should have the discipline to set aside certain times to do specific tasks through the day. For example, don't check your emails until you have completed task one, two and three. I would go insane and I don't think that has anything to do with the potential success of my business or not.

That's pure perception on someone's part, and someone else's viewpoint only works from where they are standing. We can't all be painted with the same entrepreneurial brush and if you can focus on one task at hand then go with it. If you can't, allow your creative mind to flow through the process of getting the job done. We've dealt with procrastination and you are beginning to know the triggers now. This part of faith is stopping the chaos in your mind and focusing your energy on more productive ways to spend your energy than panic and fear.

For the practical aspect of Focus, be sure to be present as much as possible. This is best done by doing one task at a time or leaving technology aside while you have a conversation or do grocery shopping. Stay in the moment and focus.

Acceptance

Running a business takes an immense amount of energy, which should not be used fighting against life's circumstances. The serenity prayer speaks of "accepting those things I cannot

change" for a very important reason. Resistance to the unanticipated events of life is the cause of so much stress and anxiety in our daily lives which is unavoidable in business. We count on someone paying us when they promised or a potential client calling you when they said they would, but that's not the daily reality of entrepreneurship. Taking a deep breath and accepting all the circumstances of the state of your business is one of the hardest breaths you will ever take. No one wants to accept feeling let down or disappointed. Playing the game of "what If" is equally futile and leaves you with two options. Either you're going to build up anger and resentment, ultimately destroying any glimmers of self- worth you have, or you can take responsibility for where you are and work forward from acceptance.

In the early days of Chat Factory, when we were desperate for a social media client - to at least be able to add one to the book and the business profile - we were approached by a listed company. We knew they had budget, but they told us they were limited for marketing spend for the remainder of the year and could only afford to pay us just over half the amount we quoted them. In the same breath, they assured us this was temporary and the budget for the following financial year was set for us to get our full fee. Emails went back and forth, and we all agreed on the lower fee for the next six months.

I gave my all to the client, while Greg and I looked forward to a healthy retainer and all we could do with it after the initial years of financial struggle. Needless to say, when it was time for the client to negotiate the promised contract, we couldn't pin them down for a meeting no matter how hard we tried. Stupid and naïve were just two words I used to describe myself when I realised, they had played us. I felt my energy shift into fighting the scenarios of what I could have or should have done differently, all the while my time and focus were needed in my business to recover from the financial blow. "It is what it is!" I hate that saying, because the truth of it takes away any wasted energy our ego wants to plough into being pissed off that life didn't go according to plan. Accept it!

There is a gentle process of allowing the disappointment and giving yourself time to wallow or be angry or afraid. Don't fall into the trap of seeking refuge in the positivity movement before first accepting the situation exactly as it is. Stop trying to figure out why it happened to you and accept that it has. Then, take a deep breath and go back to focusing.

Intention

Business is cutthroat and there are fewer original ideas than ever before, with everyone concerning themselves with trying to understand and outwit the competition. Entrepreneurship is not about choosing a service offering because you can ideally do something better than the next person. Having your own business is about knowing you can offer something unique, despite the competition.

Every action has a reaction and your business requires understanding of the intention behind every business move you make. There is no analysis required in this unconscious approach to decision making. Within this third breath of faith, allowing your intentions to be felt without thought, will help strip away the fears causing you to make the wrong business choices.

In a world where corruption is the norm and scams have caused immeasurable mistrust, make it your karmic choice to operate from pure intention. In this case, intention and integrity are cut from the same cloth. It may take you longer to get there if you keep your business's nose clean, but the payoffs are potentially far more rewarding.

My dad was a great wheeler and dealer, which was passed down the family tree and filtered into my first two businesses. I didn't know any better than to take the short cut, pay the additional money to the guy outside of working hours and sneak expenses under the radar. Everyone does it. Despite rationalising it into survival mode of business practice, deep down I knew it was bad business karma. My father didn't have a track record of successful businesses either, which should have been the red flag. I was thrown a lifeline in 2009, when I became partners with a very different kind of businessman. Brought up by a chartered accountant and a schoolteacher, Greg had a very different take on business and anything but straight down the line was foreign to him. In the early days he would have to rein me in and remind me that the long way around may be scarier and costlier, but it would pay off in the end. He instilled a new-found understanding of integrity into my life, to the point that I made it a daily practice to check in with myself. I attest most of our success to this simple yet under practiced approach to business.

Practically, ask yourself, "why?" as often as possible and feel your response. If the intention is pure, then there won't be a trace of fear or the need to justify your actions. You will be operating from a place of faith and taking the road less travelled to success.

Trust

Some of our greatest disappointments in life come from other people letting us down. We feel betrayed and lay the blame on others because we trusted them. When it comes to heartbreak, we find comfort in mending a broken heart, but betrayal in business can very often result in financial chaos. The reality is, everyone is out for themselves and unlike personal relationships, there doesn't have to be a level of loyalty towards entrepreneurs. Trust works three ways: trusting those around you, being trustworthy to others and trusting yourself. The latter forms the relationship within your breaths of business faith.

Mastering consciousness and trusting your intuition is a game changer in business because while others are number crunching, you're feeling your connection with the potential client or work. It may sound far too conventional, but the more entrepreneurs I speak to, the greater emphasis I see in them learning the lesson of trusting their intuition. We all learn this the hard way, but I often get told that they had a feeling it wasn't a good idea, or their instinct was to say no, but they needed the client. This is a tough breath to take and even tougher to use as the decision maker in your business. If you tell the more analytically-minded people that you felt your way through negotiations, they may tell you you're committing business suicide. You're not and you should trust yourself to believe this way of decision making.

The trust goes one step further, in trusting the flow of life and affirming your acceptance that everything is as it should be. In late 2014, I was asked to drop my fees for a smaller business and at the time we needed the additional retainer. It would have taken the edge off worrying about money for at least 6 months. However, when I met with the potential client, which was a non-profit organisation, they were demanding and in negative charity mode, still trying to negotiate the fee down even further. I sat in the meeting and felt uneasy about taking on the work, but I quickly rationalised it away because of my confidence in social media and my track record of client relations. I told myself I could do this, and it would be good for business.

It wasn't. The client was exactly as I had intuitively anticipated - they were a high maintenance nightmare! They demanded more time than we had allocated, treated myself and my employees badly and constantly equated their fee to what we were offering, which from our perspective was at a steal. The emotional drain was more timewasting than the demand from the client, because having to fire your first client is not fun. Being a charity made it even more uncomfortable, but the detriment to my business outweighed the discomfort.

My staff members were showing the strain and I couldn't risk losing them. The workload was also making it impossible to find any other clients, but the bank balance was looking healthy. Which stress is worse? Most people say it's the financial stress they would avoid at any cost, but finding trust in yourself and the power of manifestation can change all of that. Needless to say, because the universe rewards bravery, firing the client opened the floodgates of time and opportunity for Chat Factory.

In the practical process of trust, do your background checks on potential clients and offers. Avoid the hundreds of stories of fraud and being caught in scams by not shying away from getting a feel of the type of company dynamic, before embarking on a working relationship with them. Practice trusting your intuition with smaller decisions and be conscious of the impact your intuitive choices make in your business.

Happiness

What makes you happy is usually a question for all other areas of your life. 'What are you good at' is asked in the context of your career path. Although happiness has a definition, the feeling can only be experienced, and it has the potential to become the fuel which drives you through all the milestones of your business. There will be times when the work is less than thrilling, but the passion drives you through it and you will be confronted with other times when payment for your time is non-existent, but you are thrilled by every moment of work.

"But are you having fun?" is our go- to question when my team and I get together. Unlike going to a doctor, potential clients always attempt to negotiate fees down or expect more service delivery than you accounted for, and if you look at it as black and white, you'll believe there is a cut-off point that must be adhered to. Without completely overcompensating, there is a happiness allocation which every entrepreneur should count into their day. The services we offer are rarely so unique that the competition can't offer a better price and have your client throw you to the curb. Happiness has been the glue which has kept my longstanding relationships with most people in the business world. The passion and fun I have, has proven to be infectious and my employees and clients feel it.

While taking your happiness breath, the purpose is to check in and feel if you are having fun, working from happiness and doing what you love and not just what you're good at.

As an entrepreneur, I'm constantly asked if I love what I do. The answer is a passionate, YES! I have cried buckets of tears over the admin of business and there are days when throwing in the towel and opting for a set salary is beyond tempting. That part of my day is not fun. Inevitably dropping the ball does not make me happy. I hate dealing with the finances of the business and the tax man is not in my friend circle, but I don't confuse those "have -to" elements of entrepreneurship with the fact that I get to live the life I chose because I am free from corporation boundaries.

There is nothing practical about happiness. It is pure feeling, so the final breath of faith is enough to begin the process again and motivate you to focus, accept, stay within integrity and trust the process. Doing your happiness compass visualisation has the potential to become a strong guiding force, if you allow yourself to have faith in the process.

Getting practical about developing business faith, should begin with the simple mindfulness of being still. A racing mind does not master faith, even if we believe the overload of thoughts to be in the best

interest of the business. The phrase, "silence is golden", is filled with hidden messages of the impact silencing the mind can have on our lives. Quieting the mind is the ultimate form of faith, with the rewards of clearer messaging filtering through to you between the gaps of silence.

I used to trip myself up all the time and allow my mind to wander with the noise of my thoughts, instead of quieting my mind. Although I was in a state of quiet meditation, I convinced myself that I found clarity because the noise of my head was coming through as messages from my unconscious. No, that's still overthinking it, even if you believe yourself to be a master meditator. Entrusting fearless faith in your choices for your business comes from a place of absolute stillness of the mind.

If you are not comfortable with the concept of meditation, then consider this to be the simple task of finding stillness for a few moments. Don't label the process beyond giving yourself permission to relax and breathe while the rest of the world bustles along.

Get comfortable, where you know you won't be disturbed and begin to focus on your breathing. Take deep breaths in and exhale as much air out of your body as possible, then do that again and one last time. If you are used to the teachings of breathing in calm and breathing out anger or frustration, I suggest you consider what we have learned about the law of attraction. What you put out into the world is what will come back to you, yes? Then don't breathe out anger, if you are hoping for calm in return. Instead, breathe in calm and breathe out calm, then breathe it in again and

imagine it coming back to you tenfold. This is from one of the oldest Celtic beliefs of only putting out into the world what you would want in return. Choose to breathe in and out with love, calm, joy, happiness, abundance and any other energy you need to bring stillness to yourself in the moment.

Once you are relaxed, focus on one distinct sound you can hear around you. Whether it's the traffic, a chirping bird or the ticking of a clock, make sure it holds your attention. Then focus on one sensation in your body, from the feeling of your fingers making contact with the floor or the beating of your heart. Lastly, connect to the taste that is lingering in your mouth and combine all three sensations to dispel thought.

As soon as your mind wanders, go back to focusing on your breath and then the sound, followed by the sensation and lastly the taste. If you are concerned about time, set your alarm for ten minutes, so you can be at ease.

When you are ready, begin your first breath of FAITH, breathing in focus and then exhaling with focus, then with acceptance followed by intention, trust and happiness. Don't distract yourself with what each of the words meant to you in the moment. You can consciously work through that. For these five breaths, merely feel yourself filling your body, mind and energy with the elements of faith. If your mind wanders, go back to focusing on the sounds and feelings and then start back at the first breath of faith again.

When you are ready, slowly become aware of your surroundings again and carry on with your day.

Discovering your own understanding of business faith will be an empowering part of the success, but the stumbling block is the perceived lack of time. Finding a few moments, a day is filled with the energy of commitment, which is more powerful in the law of attraction than what you are even committing to.

6

WORK VS. ENERGY

Energy is the creator of all things. We learned this in science 101 and despite it being my least favourite subject, the theory of gravity has always stuck with me. We don't have to see its mechanics or understand it, to believe it. No matter what theory scientists or conspiracy theorists have about energy, they can't argue that we are surrounded and impacted by it. The energy you put in, is going to determine the results you get out and that includes success and prosperity.

Albert Einstein says it like it is, "Everything is energy and that's all there is to it. Match the frequency of the reality you want, and you cannot help but get that reality. It can be no other way. This is not philosophy. This is physics."

There's no taking the moral ground when it comes to entrepreneurship. We go into business to make money and if everything is energy, then the bucks you make are a direct result of the energy you put into making it. The hiccup comes in when entrepreneurs confuse the types of energy and think it's the mad slog, when it's actually the conscious energy you exude into the universe.

Unfortunately, most people are unconscious about the energy they are working from and can't figure out why they aren't seeing their success unfold, even when they are doing what they love. Slogging makes you exhausted, no matter how much you try convincing yourself that you're pushing hard work and passion into your business, you are only shoving exhaustion and the true energy of negative vibes into what you created with such passion. If, from the get-go, you started your business born from frustration or anxiety, then that's the energy you're pouring into it. The more we slog, the less money we make, and the cycle perpetuates, only causing heightened frustration and negative energy.

This, all to make money? I can spin any story I like, about how much passion I have for my business, but I have had to let go of some things I would love to do because they didn't become a money machine for me. #FollowSA is one of them.

I was being flown around South Africa, hosting events in every major city and networking up a storm for people. The natural people connector in me was having a field day, but you can't pay the bank by asking the manager if he'd like free sundowners while I introduced him to potential clients. The moment it started to drain my energy and I couldn't carry on the fight to figure out ways of getting people to pay me to do what I loved, I knew it was time to let go. No one reiterates to an entrepreneur that their ideas may not work. It's all about pushing through and creating more brainstorming ideas or throwing more money at it until it bankrupts you. It may never become what you envisioned because you either didn't want it badly enough from the beginning, or someone else told you it would be a good idea, or you decided on it out of fear. There's not much self-help support which guides you on when to let go, so we fight on, oblivious to the fact that we simply have to focus on either accepting or changing our energy.

Business media tosses the word 'passion' around, like it's supposed to buy us our success. They sell passion as if it's a formula you can work on, but the moment things don't fall into place, there's no solution to that unworkable formula. That's because passion equates to the energy born of physics. Hard work is not the same energy as passionate energy.

It goes wrong the very first time you don't agree with the direction life is taking your business. Control kicks in and you ask the dreaded question, "why"? Think of a time you worked for a boss, or imagine what it would be like. You are commissioned with a task and told to run with it. However, the first move you make is questioned by your boss. They want to know why you made that specific choice and what your planned outcome is from that move. Well, you were told the outcome by your boss, weren't you? Doesn't your boss trust that you would be working towards the end result set out for you? Being micromanaged would drive you crazy, right? If you have any expectation from life, your dreams, vision board, imagination, hopes, wishes or prayers, then you believe there is collaboration between you and them. You entrust your plans in whatever form, from a wish to a prayer, and then you send it out into the world to bring it back as reality.

Stop trying to boss the universe around. Stop micromanaging. Go back to chapter four and practice more faith because the only concern you should have is making sure you're doing your job with the right energy. That energy is the voice you send to the universe, reassuring life that it's getting it right and moving you in the direction you instructed it to from the beginning.

If that's not bad enough, you then get bossy again and start worrying about the "how's"? Worrying about the how's is like stopping your workforce and calling an emergency strategy meeting. Every time, you're halting your own process and placing your energy in the wrong places. Entrusting someone with a task and then not trusting the steps they would take to ensure the outcome of the success, is a sign of lack of trust in the person. No one wants to work with someone who doesn't trust them, not even the universe. Instead, just like an employee, energy will become frazzled and you will aimlessly wander until you're ready to stick to your job and let life do its job.

If you can master the art of not worrying about how it's going to pan out and focus on how you can productively use the precious hours in your day, you will bring any business plan to fruition. You are already giving your energy away somewhere. Unfortunately, it's usually manifested into stress, frustration and fear. The Universe works on the vibration of what you put out there at any time, but it uses your initial vibration as the direction to move in. This happens because you are the most conscious and clear when you take a brave step or make a bold change.

There is a distinct shift in your energy, whether you are conscious of it or not, the cogs kick into motion and move you in the direction of that energy. When you begin a business, there's excitement and enthusiasm which you pump into all your thoughts, so the universe heads you in that direction. As your feelings change, due to stress and fears, you confuse the messaging, but the universe will continue to move towards the energy of the highest and happiest vibration.

You can't control it when someone doesn't pay you your fee on time, but you can control the energy with which you respond to the financial chaos that situation may cause. Instead of purely controlling your energy toward the situation, you focus on why and then panic about how, while the universe gleefully continues to tug you in the direction of your happiness. The only one who thinks you aren't getting it right, is you. From fear, comes panic, and then the need to control the uncontrollable - life. That's the only thing you don't have control over. When you do this, you cause your own chaos.

Chaos triggers survival mode and we aren't destined to merely survive as an entrepreneur. It's a brave decision to go out on your own and make your own money, so blindly accepting survival mode should not be an option. At some point, we have to explore the extent of our capacity to believe. Your physical senses and rational thinking should be used for the daily running of your business, but it's our human right, which is built into our DNA to explore and question our potential. The conscious exploration of energy is the key to unlocking the floodgates of success, despite life's circumstances.

When you can't pay the bills, you forget the good within you and around you. It feels like too much effort to shift an attitude, but most people will push themselves harder and exhaust themselves, to no avail. It's much simpler to work on changing the energy of a situation, than controlling the outcomes, which you cannot control anyway. If you could, the world would be a perfect place and where's the adventure in that? There's so much wonder in who you are, you are your own best discovery. When your passion drives you through the chaos and into success, you uncover a newfound characteristic you didn't know you had. As entrepreneurs we need to protect ourselves from overlooking the small successes. This is only achieved by the root of almost any master's teaching: find the gratitude.

It may seem overrated because gratitude has been the buzz word for most motivational posters. Again, if it were so easy to do, then why does the world seem as though it's in mayhem and the majority of people can't count the things, they are grateful for on one hand? We start off by being grateful, then we read the self-help book in desperation. We do a few gratitude exercises or write down the things we are grateful for after a weary day, yet nothing changes.

The next morning, we wake up with a little less optimism in purely finding gratitude and the day is a trail of calamities again, so we don't waste our time being grateful at all. We tell ourselves it's silly and it doesn't work. The other scenario we are familiar with is giving up on gratitude because "bad things" happen, no matter how grateful or positive we are. I'm still trying to find the source of information who said being grateful, positive or living in faith would protect you from anything bad happening. Gratitude is not a barter deal with the universe. It is also not processed through the head. Self-help hasn't been very helpful in supporting the case of gratitude, when the mechanics have become to process gratitude instead of feeling it. Feeling it is the energy which fuels anything, and thinking it is like a speed bump when you are driving in a racing car.

My life changed when I was introduced to a different kind of universe, that of Mike Dooley, the creator of 'Notes from the Universe'. It was early 2011. I know this because I still have the note I created in his seminar. It will forever remain on my achievement board, which you hopefully created in chapter three. In the workshop he kept reiterating the importance of feeling the gratitude and not just saying it or writing it down. If you have embarked on any level of personal growth, you must have done the exercise of ending your day by making written notes of all you were grateful for during that day. I used to do that. I have books filled with them. I even continued writing in them for a few years after processing the message I had taken from Mike that day. I went through the day searching for things to be grateful for.

Some days it was a little easier, but my business was broke and all I had to go on was sticking with the gratitude. I was receiving the daily Notes from the Universe and was getting more frustrated at doing what I was told to, but still not finding my way out of the financial mess. My business partner, Greg, and I would sit for hours and contemplate our beliefs, because we were both in a space of gratitude and ending our days keeping track of all we could be grateful for. I always imagine the universe getting bored, waiting for me to figure out how to get gratitude right, so life threw me a bone. Lifeology landed its first retainer client at the beginning of 2012 and I had my first true experience of gratitude.

Overcome with excitement and relief, I remember running to the bathroom in my home, closing the door, covering my mouth and screaming at the top of my lungs. A surge of gratitude raced through me. I couldn't contain the urge to jump around, punch the air, internally scream the words "woo hoo" and then I threw my arms around myself and patted myself on the back. I hadn't felt that level of excitement since, yes you guessed it, I decided to turn my passion into my career.

I never wrote in my gratitude books again. I didn't wait until the end of the day to count my blessings either. I can tell you countless stories of dashing off to a public bathroom or dashing to my car, heading home sooner than later and allowing the surge of gratitude to catapult me further into my success story. Some days, I'm grateful for the simple repetition of having the retainer client, so I whisper, "thank you" as I walk into their offices. Then there are the awful days, when it feels as though the wheels are going to come off and my fears creep in. It calls for more awareness, but something always happens that I can be grateful for. A compliment, an enquiry or even using my network of people and introducing people is something to be grateful for. The glass is not half empty. There is no such thing as half empty glasses. Every glass is half full. Always.

> ***This practice has a name. It's called getting okay with what you've got. It starts off with getting rid of the expectation that things change drastically overnight or that gratitude will protect you from any future failures or disappointments. Gratitude is like physical exercise, building your stamina and strength, pushing you to achieve more and creating undeniable results.***
>
> ***Give yourself permission to be surprised, amazed and excited about the daily occurrences in your life. Begin with the simple gesture of whispering, "thank you". That thank you belongs to you and all the forces of life which helped you get there, so don't focus it in any specific direction, merely feel it. Feel the gratitude, in the moment, a phone call or having money to put fuel in your car. When you don't have enough money for fuel, be grateful that you have a car. If you don't have a car, be grateful that you have a public transport system. If you don't have that, be grateful for the lift or for the legs you have to walk on. If you can't be grateful for any of that my suggestion is that you should be considering some form of professional help, because there is a difference between fear and mental depression or anxiety.***
>
> ***Eventually, something slightly more exciting will***

happen, which calls for some hand clapping, jumping up and down and screeching, "woo hoo". I don't physically yell at the top of my lungs, because that could be cause for some concern when in public bathrooms. I do hold my hand over my mouth and silently yell, sometimes until I feel a tingle or blood rushing to my cheeks.

In April 2015, I ticked one of my biggest dreams off my list. All my gratitude and conscious maintaining of energy led my business to great success and I was able to pay for a trip to the United States and chase after my love for country music. Being a South African, we don't get any American country music, except for the few artists who go mainstream at which point I'm over them anyway. In Nashville, the pulse of country music, I visited the Grand Ole' Opry, where every person who has ever meant anything to country music stood in one specific spot on the Opry stage.

I'm wiping tears of gratitude away as I reminisce and share that moment with you. I had nowhere to sneak off to, so I publicly wept my way through the tour. I was with one of my best friends and she got what the moment meant to me, so we didn't say a word to each other. The tears were filled with woo hoo's and thank you's. I felt gratitude surge through me and at the moment when I stood in the very spot that stars like Johnny Cash had stood, I knew I could achieve anything by purely being grateful. To this day, the picture of me standing on the stage of the Grand Ole' Opry is the only framed photo in my home.

I can't say when it will happen or how you will feel, but the moment will come when you will have to drop everything and race to a place where no one can see you jump around, throw your hands in the air and ooze gratitude the way it was meant to be used, as a tool of physics and the creation of unlimited success.

If the gratitude exercises seem crazy, take a look at the number of hours you think you need to put in, to create success for yourself. Which one is crazier?

The greatest destroyer of our energy flow is exhaustion, which is common in the overworked entrepreneur. I know this from personal experience and taking all the wrong advice about what an entrepreneur's life should look like. Facebook posts from others like me, showing the world they are working harder than anyone else and that they are proud not to have a life, but to call themselves their own boss. 'Work now so you don't have to later', is the mantra of most entrepreneurs, but there is no defining guideline of how much work it takes. I've read all the books guiding us to work now and have the life of a millionaire when we are retired, but by then we have missed all the precious moments and the majority of us won't become as wealthy as the books promise.

In 2010, after pushing myself to the limits of entrepreneurship, my body was begging me to stop. I had done physical work, as a massage therapist, until 2008 and replaced that with sitting behind a computer and manically doing anything possible to find work and get the attention of anyone who would pay us. I fiercely wrote blog posts and spent hours creating content I could share with the world. Working through the night because the next day was the promise of more potential, I convinced myself that money wasn't coming in because I wasn't showing up each day with enough passion. We don't have the luxury of a weekend and we certainly don't go on holiday. I had lunch with two successful entrepreneurs in late 2009 and they made the process of making money sound torturous. Whatever I said about doing what I loved, the one would respond with the question, "but are you making money?" I wasn't. He never backed that up with a solution, so like every other struggling entrepreneur, I assumed it meant I had to work harder.

By May 2010 I was struggling to get through the day without severe back pain and self-diagnosed myself as lazy. I spent way too much time behind the computer, so I had to get myself moving. I didn't have much time for gym, so I would climb on the treadmill and run for as long as I could. Some days I was exhausted, so it was only ten minutes, but other days I pushed myself to get my body moving as much as I pushed to keep it sitting still. By July, the chiropractor, physiotherapy and painkillers hadn't helped, so I went for x-rays.

By that stage I could hardly walk and couldn't drive properly because lifting my leg to press the brake took too much effort. It didn't stop me though and I would use my mother's automatic car to get around. In early August, I woke up to indescribable pain. I was immobile and literally yelped for help until my mother heard me. The saving grace was my decision, however humbling at the time, to move home in order to cut costs when I started Lifeology. If I had been alone that day, I have no idea how I would have managed to get help. Ambulances, wheelchairs, cortisone injections under anaesthetic and nearly two months of being unable to walk was the result of striving to be a successful entrepreneur.

From all the hours of sitting, lack of time to slowly exercise my body and pure exhaustion of every muscle and bone in my body, my spine gave in on me. L3 and L4 are the lower disks of the spine, which collapsed on each other under pressure. It trapped a nerve down my leg and left me immobile and in excruciating pain for long enough to rethink the entire theory of burning the candle at both ends.

By October I was walking again and proudly managed to keep up my daily Project Me blogging, except for two days when the pain was just too much and Greg had to blog for me.

The blog post read: "Jo's back has taken her down and the drugs have made her delirious, so this is Greggie writing yesterday's entry for her.

My dear friend is being a champ through all of this and sticking to her "Project Me" principles. She is working on putting herself first, listening to her body and has done what is necessary to help her body through this ordeal. She has endured extreme pain for days.

I was in the fortunate position of looking after Jo yesterday while her family celebrated her sister's birthday. We spent a special few hours on her bed together watching two of our favourite movies, Under the Tuscan Sun and Priscilla, Queen of the Desert. The former had us in tears – special healing and cleansing tears.

The underlying message really hit home: always follow your heart, no matter what your mind thinks. Oh, and then there is the beautiful analogy of hunting ladybugs, then giving up and falling asleep in the grass only to wake covered in them. Patience, self-love, ladybugs and dreams of a holiday villa in Tuscany: these are what carry Jo through times like this ... and you, of course."

I arose from that ordeal a changed entrepreneur. I became conscious that hard work does not make you a success. The combination of passion, self-respect and hard work make you a success. I replaced the candle I burned at both ends for the candles I use to meditate daily. No matter how many clients need my attention, or emails wait to be answered and how demanding my day gets, there is always time for me. I dropped all the excuses and spent most of my days working through the guilt of consciously making time for me. Yes, you'll be riddled with guilt. You'll panic that the time you took to go to the movies instead of answering emails will be detrimental to your business. It's as if we imagine an entrepreneurial gremlin waiting to grab our assets the second, we turn our back away from work and towards us.

Balance is my least favourite cliché. Balancing takes equally hard work as being out of balance and it guides us to juggle all the balls we already have, then add "me time" as an additional ball. It's not balance we are looking for, but detachment. When you're working, give it your all, but then put the balls down. Detach from working and swap the juggling balls for a fun, coloured beach ball. Play, in whatever form that means to you, then know when you need to focus on work again. When you're balancing, you will quickly check your mobile phone while dropping the kids at school or answer an email while pushing your trolley in the supermarket. Detachment doesn't mean abandonment. It also doesn't need any stringent rules, because the energy you put into being detached is as important. If you do it riddled with anxiety, you may as well be working.

My time is demanded from early in the day, with Chat Factory staff and clients messaging me from as early as 7am. Social media comes alive and I am ready for it the moment the majority of my world wakes up. My daytime hours have very little detachment and I have learned to love the demand on my time during those hours. At sunrise, I detach from everything. It's no more than half an hour, but I wake up, sip on one of my favourite flavoured teas and sit quietly with the sunrise. I detach from everything except me and then my day begins.

My exercise time is exactly the same and the simplest of all is the escape to the kitchen to cook to a country music song. You will not find me with my laptop while cooking, even if I'm only scrambling an egg for myself. You also will not find my phone in my hand while a song plays. I'm famous for taking five minutes. When I introduce a new staff member to the team, I describe the work environment and give them the rundown on what it means when I say I need five minutes. Moments of detachment during the day are not impossible to take. They are bite size moments of stepping away from the busy-ness.

Here are some ideas to help you find ways to detach.

Regardless of whether or not you're an entrepreneur, finding time for you is vital. Being a parent, a caregiver, a sportsperson, or whatever takes up your time when there is no detachment, something has to suffer and it's always going to be you.

Begin by leaving your phone in another room or out of reach. When there are responsibility restraints, like family, give your phone to someone else or set a special ringtone for family only. Do simple chores without any attachment to work. Make and drink your cup of coffee,

cook, catch up on the news the old fashioned way and never shop while scrolling through your phone. These moments of detachment are the human way of recharging our batteries and maintaining the energy flow we need to keep our lives on track and in rhythm with our plans.

The ultimate of all is to take a nap. When you stop getting in your own way and shut down your thoughts, you reset yourself into the full space of possibility, so go and take a nap.

Although these bite size moments or 'five minutes' are great, there needs to be more substantial time to detach from work and plug into you. Get your journal out and make a list of the hobbies or things you love to do, which are neglected due to time constraints. Make sure there is some form of exercise or getting outdoors in the mix. Moving your body is vital for energy flow. Now you get to work on making time for secret appointments.

You don't have to tell your clients, employees or friends when you mark off a meeting while booking a revitalising massage or take yourself to lunch. If finances are an issue, go home, read a book and detach. When it's impossible to escape from work, rely on the people around you to allow this time. Ask your spouse if you can have an hour to bath and even though it's after hours, still write it in your diary. The consciousness of making time for yourself is a key part of this daily practice. Yes, you will need to do this daily. You don't have to be extreme and book out major appointments for an hour, but even if you struggle to usually find time to do the groceries or make breakfast,

mark it as an appointment for the following day. People always ask me how I am so busy but still seem to be having fun and loving what I do. The secret is out. I make appointments with fun so as never to return to being the painful reverse of a self-inflicted workaholic.

7

SELF-WORTH VS. FINANCIAL WORTH

Money, in essence, is nothing. In its tangible form, it's made from paper or melted metal. It's even less tangible now, because not much physical money exchanges hands. The world around us decides its value and in some parts of the world, currency is an animal or a hand crafted piece of furniture. The crafter may see much more value in his masterpiece than a bank account filled with money, which in reality is filled with nothing.

When I was a little girl, I had a piggy bank. I also had one of the first ATM cards, which was aimed at teaching us to save. Before that though, I had an account at the post office, which is totally giving my age away, but let's move swiftly along. When it was time to move my money from the post office to the bank, my dad helped me along the process. I thought he would need to help me carry my coins to the bank, in the same way that he had helped me carry them from my piggy bank to the post office. That didn't happen. There were a few pieces of paper which needed signing and then the banging sound of the stamp slamming confirmation on the magical transfer of my precious coins from one institution to another.

I will never forget being boggled at the farce that I was sure was taking place before my very eyes. I wanted my coins back. I wanted my exact coins back, because that's why I gave them to the post office - for safekeeping. My dad wasn't great at being serious, so he went about teaching me money lessons by telling me it grew on trees. He went as far as dropping coins all around one of my favourite trees in the garden and told me the leaves turned to notes, which grew into coins and then fell to the ground for us to pick up.

As I grew older and money issues crept into my father's reality, his tune changed and my parents would throw out comments like, "money doesn't grow on trees." I preferred his scenario of it growing on trees and in my adult life, have a much-appreciated respect for the lesson I believe my dad wished he could have taught me.

I grew up with a tragically skewed perception of anything money-related, as my father went from being a millionaire to a pauper time and again. The only reason we moved to a new house was when we packed up to live in something far grander and more elaborate and then packed up again to squish into something hardly affordable. My life went from picking which car my dad should use on a Sunday drive to watching the cars being auctioned off from my bedroom window. Being my father's daughter didn't benefit my relationship with money either, because everything was about barter and having the gall to expect never to pay full price for anything.

One of the main reasons I needed counselling and spiritual guidance was to rectify my relationship with money. The contradiction in our upbringing was stark.

I didn't realise it was a relationship back then and took it as a means to an end. That's so cliché, but it is ingrained in the psyche of most of us. We have to make money. We will be bitterly miserable without it. We could potentially be suicidal without it because we aren't worth anything without it.

Although money is at the forefront of the reason, we begin a business in the first place, I consciously chose to deal with it as I neared the end of the book. Don't fool yourself or anyone else around you that you started your business purely out of passion. If it were the old days and you could trade your crafty cupcakes for someone else's supply of egg, that would be ideal, but you can't drop a batch of cookies at the bank manager. We go into business for money. However, we don't make money purely from doing business.

Before the currency of money, there was barter system of tools to slaughter animals in exchange for the meat or wood, and stone in exchange for the weapon. The history of money will go on to explain that the length of time became an issue for some traders, so they would create IOU (I owe you) notes. Those notes would be passed along from one person to another, as they all began to owe each other.

However, our concern as entrepreneurs, is about the energy exchange that existed way before money was even an imagined idea. The traders saw value in and appreciated the time and effort it took for their fellow trader to produce the goods they needed. Someone was digging for stones while the other was cutting crops and another was feeding and herding animals. So back to the essence of money: they were trading energy. Going one step further, if you accepted my reference to Albert Einstein's, "everything is energy and that's all there is to it," theory, then money is energy too. Simply, money is pure energy. Energy has nothing to do with how hard you work, but the energy in which you work, and so we have opened the floodgates to a new relationship with money and wealth.

When you think of your current financial situation, what feelings stir in your body? It's a good idea to close your eyes and try really feel what money is currently doing to your energy. Is your body riddled with resentment or unsettled with fear? Are you in denial and can't bring yourself to do the exercise? Taking deep

breaths, let's go back to one of the basic holistic steps to entrepreneurship.

Tell yourself the truth about your current relationship with money. If this brings up a lot of fear or anger, don't hold back on the emotions because the truth behind it will be the catalyst to change it. When you're ready, write your current feelings about money in your journal. Get it all out and don't sugar coat it. If you hate it or resent it or are bitter that others have it, get it all out of your system and really feel your current energetic connection to it.

Are you concentrating? Because the next sentence could be your wealth game-changer. Read it at least five times before moving on: Money issues are NOT about money.

Money, as pure energy, is merely the pawn in the game you created for yourself. What is the point of doing anything without a reward - and the entrepreneurial rewards are perceived to be getting up and doing what you love everyday - but it's really about the money. Like the game of monopoly, you move a piece along the board and get frustrated when the dice doesn't take that piece to where you would like it. In life, your choices are like a roll of the dice and money is moved along, usually landing where you don't want it to. If you want the game to change, you have to shift the energy with which you are playing it. None of us can control what will be thrown at us, but we can take control of our outcome by shifting our energy and consciously creating situations that will create abundance, no matter what life throws at us.

Money is fuelled with the outcome you set for yourself and is always moving you along the direction that you set your energetic compass to. Money doesn't care if you buy a house or a Ferrari with it. It's only governed by the energy with which you work towards it and accept the loss or gain of it. Referring back to setting our compass to happiness in chapter three, money becomes the obstacle along the way to ensure you stay on track. We spend our lives fighting this battle against money, meanwhile its energetic purpose is to keep us on the very path we set out for ourselves.

When you have long forgotten to cling to your self- worth or life purpose, there money is, clutching on for you. It knows your hidden gifts and greatest strengths aren't going to be found down the path of losing your identity or selling out, so it doesn't give you enough to make those low esteem choices for yourself. The cycle perpetuates when we become obsessed with fixing the money problems and not focusing on what we need to develop or change within ourselves. The hours spent reshuffling budgets or rethinking business plans are futile if those choices aren't moving you in the direction of your happiness. Money knows that and it's up to you as to how long it takes for you to figure that out.

The other factors which impact money and will cause financial chaos, until we consciously practice it, are:

- Not working within your discovered self-worth
- Succumbing to your ego's fearful voices
- Avoiding decisions made in low self esteem
- Relinquishing responsibility
- Operating outside of integrity
- Not telling yourself the truth
- Focusing on money
- Denying your purpose
- Not having fun

Through the past weeks or months of working through conscious entrepreneurship, you should be familiar with a few triggers for financial chaos. Remember that it's not necessary to go back to the drawing board and try figure out new lessons. Our patterns have been repeating for years and the mere acknowledgement of a specific cause of money chaos will already begin to start making the obstacle more obvious.

There are no more tools to be dished out to you. From here, you are armed with everything you need to remain conscious and focused along your path to entrepreneurial happiness. At the end of the book is a recap of the imaginings and journal work, which you should have been practicing. By now, much like exercise, your conscious fitness should be ready to tackle your relationship with money.

I keep mentioning the word, "relationship", have you noticed that? In my world and the one I am helping you create now, there is a very intimate and committed relationship with money. Let me begin by defining intimacy for you. Within a relationship between two people, there is a level of trust which allows one or both parties to drop the veil of insecurity and shame and truly be vulnerable in that relationship. Intimacy is not about getting naked in the dark, but about having the lights on and allowing all the flaws and fears to show. The same applies to your relationship with money, because you are going to form one. When we are not open with someone else and we avoid letting them in wholly and completely, mistrust will always be the underlying foundation. We get very confused with where the responsibility of intimacy lies and almost everyone has said to their partner, "you don't make me feel comfortable". That is unfair to another human being because the space of being vulnerable is purely our own responsibility. If you aren't feeling safe enough to show your true self, there is something within you that is lacking. It may be that you are ignoring the voices trying to warn you not to trust the other person, but the onus is still on you. Although I feel a relationship book brewing, this isn't it, so let's get back to your vulnerable relationship with money.

Imagine the momentum of energy where every action has a reaction. When something is driven by energy and gains speed, eventually it will soar like a plane. It could equally sink like a submarine. Relationships have the same energy. It is the transfer of energetic emotion or respect which determines the health of a relationship. Money is also energy and you have a relationship with it, where your energetic emotion and respect will determine if it will be fruitful and loving, or trying and abusive. It is purely up to you to choose. Imagine giving money the respect it deserves, like some gratitude when it comes along. How about going to dinner and acknowledging the partnership between you and money as you pay for the bill.

In 2012, my businesses were bringing in enough money for us to make it past the crucial five-year mark. I don't know who decided what the timeline benchmarks should be, but after five years, we felt the milestone of success and ticked the box of half a decade with pride. The business had money, but I personally had no wealth to speak of. That's a polite way of saying I was broke. When running your business with longevity in mind, don't assume that any income is yours. Take my advice and allocate yourself a salary as early on as possible. This wasn't my bright idea, but that's why I chose to have a business partner. I allowed Greg to deal with the logistics of money, because I was too afraid to. Having two failed businesses and a family history of constant uncertainty with money, I didn't trust myself to manage it. Greg knew the expenses and he decided what our salary amounts would be. It wasn't a lot; we were still in the phase of having to take it from the business as it allowed for us to draw out. I could never adjust to needing anything though. In my world, money was given to you and it was whipped away from you as easily. When Greg and I met, I had hardly seen any of the world or my own country. My clothes were a necessity, most of them hand- me-downs from my siblings and I had no idea what it meant to buy myself something merely because I could. When it came to money, everything was purely necessity and there was never enough.

. . .

Before Greg resigned from his final corporate job, he booked us two tickets to Italy and Germany. I had the joy of turning 35 at Oktoberfest in Munich. We used his capital from his resignation pay-out to fund our trip and along the way he taught me the gift of always knowing we were worthy of having more than enough. I hardly enjoyed the trip, to be honest, and allowed many of my money issues to get in the way. If you ask him his version of the holiday, he will tell you if I hadn't changed my relationship with money, he would never have travelled with me again.

Back to 2012 and the most profound step I took in creating a happy and healthy relationship with money. I didn't discover everything on my own and decided to do a course to consciously improve my relationship with money. I learnt to tolerate the energy of money in a healthy way and strip away the fears and secrets. I have carried one exercise with me and use it every day of my life, which is feeling the partnership between money and myself. We are truly in it together and this chapter won't be complete without you finding that same bond with your finances. In that process, I was tasked with defining the relationship I would want with money and it is something we are going to do together, now.

This exercise is going to take you out into the world, so you may not be able to do it immediately, but as we did in the previous chapter, make a date with this process and put it in your diary. Take yourself out somewhere, where you will need to spend a little money on yourself. It doesn't have to be extravagant. Go for lunch or buy coffee and walk through the park. You need to do this alone and have your journal with you. Sit quietly with what money has just bought you and start to see money as an equal partner in your life. Now write down what you would want your money relationship to look like.

My realisation was about the trips I wanted to take with money and the joy I imagined I would experience while exploring new cities. I saw myself having adventures with money, which I could add to my achievement board. We all want our other half to unexpectedly arrive home with a bunch of flowers or an item of clothing they spotted you staring at as you strolled past the shop window. I wanted money to make sure we had a beautiful home with a view of the sunrise and the sunset, and each day I watch it from my apartment window, I thank money for the mutual bond we have with each other. In exchange, I work fearlessly and always know my current financial situation.

Prior to working on my openness with money, Greg controlled everything, I didn't even know the passwords to our bank accounts. I had never received a monthly summary of income and expense. It wasn't because there were any secrets in the partnership. It was because I genuinely didn't want to know. I had so much trust in Greg and gave him so much responsibility that I didn't have to carry any on my own. That dynamic isn't healthy in a financial relationship.

Almost instantly, as I learned everything there was to know about the business's financial state, money started to stabilize. I wrote down my contribution to the healthy partnership and promised our money to always remain aware of my financial situation.

Seeing money as a partnership is the first step in a line of scary ones that many of us have to take. The foundation of being a holistic entrepreneur is telling yourself the truth. The rose-coloured glasses should be long gone, and you should be aware that there's no such thing as wishing troubles away with positivity memes. Knowing your true financial state is vital for rebuilding a relationship with money. No secrets. Truth can be built on, but a lie cannot be sustained, and the repercussions of not being aware of both your debt and your credit is financial suicide. This is the area in which I am most frustrated regarding the advice given to aspiring entrepreneurs. The focus is on dreaming bigger and shoving pictures of unrealistic goals all over your walls, when very few are asking us if we can get by just for today. Do you know how long you can get by for financially? Not many of you do, but you will take your last pennies, in a desperate state and buy another book in the hope that it will make you rich.

I haven't used the word "rich" at all for a very specific reason. Rich is the trap. It's the word both sides of the spectrum banter around to see which team wins the most people over. The esoteric world will say you don't need to be financially rich, if you are spiritually rich, and the entrepreneurial evangelists tease you with riches beyond your wildest dreams. You don't want either of these. That old tale of being absolutely fulfilled on a soul level, but living just within your means is merely the story of the misunderstood spiritual wanderers. I say this with empathy, because when I owned my spa, I was this person; deeply on a spiritual quest and doing healing therapy, which was making other people feel so much better about their lives. I was healing and that was reward enough. Was it? It couldn't have been because I didn't have enough money to pay the bank or the rent at the end of the month. Something wasn't right and I knew it could be possible to continue to do my healing work in the world, but also be financially abundant. Now there's a word I like. If you are going to choose talks or seminars where millionaires promise a quick fix to riches, make sure you understand the difference between their form of rich and your quest for abundance. Every fairy tale explains this to us, and Disney has done a sterling job of working this massively important life realisation into the moral of the story. Someone is always rich and thinks they can have whatever they want because of it. The goal, many times, is a princess. The rich never win but the story always ends with abundance. Have you noticed that everyone who is in abundance has the best of both worlds? The princess finds love and lives in a magical castle?

In your journey towards abundance, the process of truth telling should take a few days or weeks if you are only lifting your head from the sand now. To start this exercise, let me explain what I do when I get scared. I imagine myself as a giraffe and know I have a choice between sticking my head in the sand or standing tall and having a view way above the treetops and governing my environment. It's worth having a birds' eye view, which begins by creating a full list of debtors and creditors.

There is an astounding amount of people who do not know what their credit card limit is or how much they still owe on their house or car. They don't want to know what the email says about their store cards and avoid supplier calls at the beginning of the month. If you don't have an accountant and are doing your books yourself, you need to know your standing on taxes. Not one penny can go unaccounted for, which goes for assets as well. Don't fret, when I started this exercise, I had no assets at all. Not a thing to call my own and I was in my late thirties. This isn't an exercise on how far along your path you are. It's all about getting intimate with your money situation.

I am not a financial advisor and this book isn't about how to go about paying back debt, but I strongly suggest that you do not do this process on your own. Relationships need counsellors many times and this one may need it too. You should at least have a bookkeeper, who has a neutral outlook on your income and expenses. You have to have a tax guy and if you have a large amount of debt, find yourself a debt counsellor. Focus on energy and taking loving responsibility for yourself and your money will help attract the right people to help you.

> ***Over the next few days, become aware of your feeling towards money and start to see it as a partnership. If money could speak, what do you think it would say to you about your strengths and self-worth? I can't guarantee it, but a part of me also has no doubt that universal coincidences will happen through the process. You will be put into situations which could help you shift more into your highest esteem or a conversation will trigger an idea which has the potential to become something financially worthwhile, if you are brave enough. Stop worrying about making more money and rather spend that time listening to the lessons money may be teaching you about yourself.***

This isn't going to be easy to do, but there are other things that can be done to help the process along. Do you remember the gratitude and "thank you" moments you were encouraged to create in chapter six? Now think about the last time someone gave you a gift you were grateful for. Imagine the moment of gratitude and thanking them. Over the past handful of years, I have bought everything with money as my partner.

As I hand my cash to the cashier, I whisper, "thank you" to money. I never forget the partnership we have together and know that the only reason I have the money is because of my fearless work to create it. If you can make it common practice to acknowledge money for being available to spend, you should notice a significant difference early in the process. The catch is that you have to pay debt with the same gratitude. Any amount of resentment is a reflection of that relationship.

I have a friend who is paying off debt from a failed engagement and begrudgingly pays over a sum of money to the bank for a relationship gone wrong and a marriage that never happened.

Slowly, I have helped her reframe some of the resentment into gratitude for being set free from a relationship which could have destroyed her self-worth completely. Her salary is good enough to pay the amount each month, so she ultimately has much to be grateful for. It's taken a while for her to make the payment in gratitude, but she received an increase and is paying it off much faster so that it can be put behind her sooner. Sometimes we have to dig deep to find the gratitude for money we pay begrudgingly, but the reason is there and its worth taking the time to figure it out. Not one virtual coin should move from one energy to another without gratitude.

I lived through the petrifying end of the month angst. I had the debt, the banks calling me, suppliers closing in on me and not enough money coming in to pay out what I owed. Some of the debt was old and I begrudgingly paid it across, until I reminded myself of where I would have been at that moment in my life, had I not managed to accumulate some credit from a supplier.

Living debt free is about living free of feeling indebted, which is purely a choice. Choice is the single most important aspect of life, which far outweighs what the gurus say even about love. Why? Because you still have to choose to love. Using that power to choose your financial prosperity is not found in fate or in hope. It is found in consciously working with the energy of money.

There are four pillars to prosperity, forming the invisible wall that holds up all the abundance, which is waiting to flow your way. The daily awareness of these practices are the hardest parts of the work you should do for your business.

Track your money: Whether you do it yourself or have a financial consultant or business partner, you need to know your financial situation each day. Go into your bank account and know your debt and your income. Create a daily budget or at least track your spending. I have an app on my phone and as I purchase something, I add it into the expenses while the payment is being processed. I draw out cash for parking or tips along the way and have a caring eye on my money at all times.

Asking for money owed to you: chasing money that's owed to you is not the best part of business, but it's also a task you aren't going to avoid. We all have to deal with debt and cash flow issues. No one gets away with not having to chase up money. The nature of business is that there will be someone who can't pay or has a strategic reason for paying later. Money is rightfully yours upon service delivery, but the true magnet for money is when you confidently have the courage to ask for it. If it is very uncomfortable for you, send an email and if it has been dragging on, get a debt collector, but show up for your money and fight for it.

Charge what you are worth: If your industry is anything like mine, there is no true benchmark of what should be charged for your services or expertise. As a lawyer, you are never asked for a discount and a doctor doesn't negotiate fees, but I am asked to do it on a daily basis.

When getting your business off the ground, it is understandable to keep your costs slightly lower, to

attract new customers. I did that for a while, but as soon as I landed my first client, I set the bar higher and refused to drop below my worth. At times it can be more of a feeling than figuring out your expenses and fattening it up with profit, which your accountant is going to hate. Going on gut has much to do with what you will set as your minimum fee, and trusting your intuition will help you set prices, most of the time.

Whatever you do, have a minimum and refuse to go below that. You will be surprised at how many people are willing to pay more than your lowest fee. As a tip, I always ask people what budget they have set aside and, on some occasions, it has been way more than I would have charged. I tap into my integrity and find a middle ground, time and again. Money loves that game.

Save: Even if you put away one percent of your income a month, get into the habit of saving money. It doesn't have to be to secure your future immediately or be an exorbitant amount. When getting started or in financially dire times, the last thing we believe we can do is save. I began by putting away a few hundred a month and did that for many years before I could think of saving anything substantial.

Remember, this is the energetic part of growing wealth and eventually you will need financial planners to guide you on the abundance you are able to invest and save.

Money and I have created many exciting moments together, both for the businesses and in my personal life. We have seen dreams come true and continue to stretch the imagination of future exciting plans.

We have also worked through fearful moments together, especially with the world's financial mayhem. There have been days where everything could fall apart and finances seemed as though they were dwindling away, but I always remind myself that this journey of conscious business is not to make the world of entrepreneurship easy, but to be grateful when money comes up as the teacher or catalyst to something greater.

8

FULFILMENT VS. JOY

'Do what you love, and you'll never work a day in your life.'

This statement may be the one which has turned more people's simple pleasures into financial and emotional torture. If you haven't heard of starving artist syndrome, it is associated with people who have a burning desire for their creative passion, and struggle to turn it into financial success.

Being born to do what you love is not as simple as that, because there is a deeper layer of understanding you need to have about the relationship you form with making money. If we return to everything being energy, and life having the essentials which we cannot live without and which take money to sustain, then sometimes doing what we love is not enough.

Emma was a passionate baker. She never took a baking course and wasn't born into a family where recipes had been handed down to her. There was something natural in her making and her ease for creating sugary treats was the talk of her friends and family. To bake all day was a dream of hers. On the other hand, she was really good at her day job too. Emma was an accountant and had worked her way up to managing a department in an accounting firm. The salary was good and her contribution to support her husband in taking care of their family was very rewarding.

At some point, Emma doesn't remember when, the seed was planted that she was such a good baker and she would be able to sell dozens of her cakes and eclairs in a heartbeat. She may have said it to a friend or two, and before she knew it, she couldn't get the thought out her head. Friends were getting wind of her idea to maybe sell a cake here and there. Just enough of her friends were riding the wave of; 'do what you love' and added to the rambling thoughts in her mind. Encouraging her on and telling her they would tell all their friends in town, she started to weigh up working behind a desk all day or turning her kitchen into her joyous space of baking for hours on end. Baking made her so deeply happy, which is exactly what has been fed into the collective. It's supposed to be easy. Do what you love, right?

With enough nagging and encouraging from her friends and loving support from her husband and family, Emma allowed the thoughts of being a full-time baker sink in. It never changed that she was good at her accounting career, but with each passing day, she lost her desire to go to the office.

"Do what you love, and the money will flow", had been said to her enough times to create the courage to turn her heart more to the dream of baking than the passion she did have for the career she was in.

Energy is very sensitive and not to be taken lightly. With no surprise, the energy of her workplace started to change from a joyous space to one of frustration and tension. Within a moment it seemed as though all arrows were pointing to her giving up her stable career for the life of an entrepreneur. Emma was given a tough client to handle. The compliment was that they were tough, and her boss was very aware that the role of dealing with this client was cut out for Emma's personality. It wasn't the soft baker in Emma, but the relentless woman who had worked so hard to get to the position where she was trusted with management roles in the business.

Within a few months, the client got really tough, Emma became weary and her friends leaned in to truly support her. Their support came from a loving space and the wearier she felt, the greater their support became. The encouragement was unanimous. If she was no longer doing what she loved, then she should pick something that she truly loved, and the money would be there. It had to be, because money always shows up if you just do what you love.

The story is long, but the outcome is an inevitable one when you understand that there is a difference between fulfilment and joy. Yes, we do energetically attract money. However, being an entrepreneur shifts a financial responsibility onto what we do and tests the energy with which we do it. At this point is the great misunderstanding of fulfilment and joy.

We need to work in order to make money, which fulfils the needs we have in our lives. I doubt anyone who has the luxury to live a life of a flowing income, with no need to work will have been guided to read this book. Minus the handful of people like that, we need to do something with our lives which fulfils the financial responsibilities we have.

There is a distinct balance in this fulfilment of being good at it and also having a sense of happiness and pride around it. That does not take away from the other part of our lives, which also have the ability to create money for us, being our joy. This is a new mindset in the scheme of things. Our parents and grandparents didn't financially need it or desire it, but the world is changing. Making money is not the same today as it was when we were growing up. Consolidating it to one source of energy and sticking to that energy for decades doesn't seem to have the same outcome as it used to. Today, many of us desire or need a side hustle. More than one stream of income. If we don't then it could be that the unspoken but very distinct message from the universe is that we should have it.

This is where most people get confused, stuck and then find

themselves in financial crisis. There is a difference between the money you make from fulfilment and that which you make from joy. This side hustle or the different income streams sits right here, but we are told that we don't need the money from fulfilment, and we can easily weigh all the pressure on our joy.

This is a lesson which was not easy for Emma to learn. It took her family nearly falling apart and her husband turning from being loving and supportive to financially and emotionally drained. Emma turned against her family and friends, who were the ones promising the clients would come. She ticked all the boxes for turning her joy of baking into a business. She was brave and let go of a career which no longer made her happy. The Facebook page had been set up and business cards were printed. With each thing she baked, she posted it on Instagram and used all the hashtags to draw the crowds. The crowds never came.

This is the problem with so many people who turn their joy into their fulfilment. Money has a purpose and it is linked to that which you are good at and which brings you an equal sense of fulfilment. Turning what we love, what brings us simple joy – no matter how good at it we are, into our source of fulfilment does one detrimental thing. It sucks the joy out of it.

When Emma was going to work and spending her weekends baking, while complaining about the nagging client and the seemingly lack of support from her boss, her baking made everything better. Despite creating masterpieces which only her children and husband indulged in, the simple joy of that baking had no pressure. That cake helped her find balance and restored her energy to go back into the world the following day. It did not have the financial responsibility to feed her family or contribute to the bond on the house. It was simply her joy.

Unbeknown to Emma, her boss had given her the responsibility because he could see her ability to thrive under pressure. It was far from the feelings she had in the kitchen, when she was creatively icing cupcakes. High pressure for less money than she could make if she got x number of order of cakes in x number of days. Of course, the number was inflated. When putting imaginative pressure on our joy, we all do that.

Instead of baking a leisurely cake on the weekend, Emma and her supportive friends ran the numbers and she could do two cakes and three batches of cupcakes. That might be sustainable for someone who chose the career of being a baker (and has their own form of joy) over someone who is about to drain the life and fun out of simply baking.

Fulfilment and joy are a tricky concept to get your head around, but the bottom line is that sometimes you have to stick to what you are good at and not dive into putting so much financial pressure on something which truly and deeply makes you happy. That is not to say that you can never turn your joy into fulfilment. It's usually better to rather take your time to find the balance between the two and then see if you want to eventually have all your income be the responsibility of your joy.

Of all disappointments I see in entrepreneurship, this is the one which is the hardest to get people to understand. It is the toughest for me too. My absolute joy is writing. This book is filling my soul more than you could ever begin to imagine. If I didn't deeply understand the difference between fulfilment and joy, I would easily say I was closing the doors on my social media business and turning to writing every day of my life. It's such a deep passion of mine, how could the universe not show up and let the money flow? That goes against everything we have been told about doing what we love, and the money will come. The reality is two-fold. Firstly, I'm damn good at the role I play in the social media world. Is it tough? Hell yes! Are there days I would trade it for a cabin in the mountains and the dream of speaker gigs on the odd day, because I dream of getting paid so much as a speaker. There are more days of daydreaming about that than I can count. However, if I let go of what I'm good at and turn what I love into my forced source of income, I will surely lose the joy for writing. I'm never quitting writing though, and I'm holding onto those dreams of revenue flowing in from books sold and income from speaker gigs. However, to fulfil my daily need for income, I also get to do something I am brilliant at and deeply passionate about.

The concept of fulfilment and joy took me years to figure out. I had to try support an artist friend, who gave up his business in information technology because he is a brilliant painter. It took spending hours of unpacking why his joy was not turning to a flow of money, to finally see that he had literally dropped something which he was truly good at and sucked the joy out of his art when it couldn't pay the first month's rent.

I had another woman turn to me for advice when she plucked up the courage to leave her job as a sales consultant to open a doggie grooming mobile parlour. Her joy was so deeply ingrained in her love for animals, and making sales was tough in the current economy. She wanted an easier option. Something to call her own. What better way to do it than turn her joy to her fulfilment?

Can you see what happened there? Turning your joy to your fulfilment has the implications of turning what you simply love doing into it being the source of survival. We are not meant to make money from everything we are good at. There should always be an aspect of self which is simply for the pleasure and joy of it.

I see myself slowly finding the balance between making money from my fulfilment of social media and my joy of writing. However, I have found myself a new joy. Amazingly, my friends are already (with love) nagging me to turn that joy into a way of making money too, but I have become smarter than that.

When I'm pottering around the kitchen, adapting traditional recipes to plant based, sugar free ones, I don't have the paid cooking lessons and sales of the cookbook on my mind. Instead, it's the simple pleasure of escaping into my joy and leaving the other parts of me to fulfil the financial expectations.

Here is the big BUT in the balance between fulfilment and joy. You do have to love what fulfils you. This chapter isn't giving you permission to stick in a career which you hate or in a job which is genuinely draining your soul. Many people are destined to be entrepreneurs and do successfully leave the corporate world to do it. Many try it and realise that having a fulfilling income wasn't so bad after all. The key lies in the 'why?'.

Emma's boss was thrilled to hear her voice after nearly 18 months of trying to make her baking business work. When she returned to her old joy, she finally got it. Being fulfilled doesn't mean every working day is going to be easy. Feeling drained and worn down isn't for cowards and her fighting spirit was reignited. She also gifted herself with not feeling like a quitter when she returned back to a fulfilling income. Baking became her simple joy again, but she did it with a twist. She continued to charge people for the cakes she did create after a crazy day's work.

Taking enough orders to add to the financial support she could share with her husband and having enough to spoil herself far more than she had in her life, allowed her to still be the entrepreneur. Does Emma dream of quitting her day job and baking her life away? Every single day. However, she can feel the fulfilment in doing what she is good at, which fills the spaces in between with what she loves.

This exercise might take a while to set the wheels into motion. If you can relate to Emma or myself, but still want to be that entrepreneur who pushes through to turn their joy to fulfilment, then find yourself another joy. It might seem overly simple, but the balance of energy is vital. Even if you volunteer at a place which needs a helping hand or tap into something you are naturally creative at, which will bring joy to your daily life.

On the other hand, if there is a deep struggle to find the

financial flow in what you once had the joy in doing, then consider the other ways you could do what you are good at and take that pressure off the joy.

The trickiest part of going from full-time employment to entrepreneurship is understanding the concept of fulfilment and joy. Are you the accountant who worked for a firm and has gone out on their own? I have one word for you – tenacity. There is no black or white in this formula. With the dozens of stories, I can tell you about those I know who destroyed their dreams by quitting their day jobs, there are dozens more who are success stories today.

The recipe does seem to be the same though. There was no drastic change in dropping their fulfilment all together and turning what they were joyously good at into the money-making machine. Entrepreneurship is not for the faint hearted. It is something which you have to ask yourself whether you are risk averse enough for, and then rest is up to tenacity.

Ask yourself, how risk averse am I? I took this question from one which came to me while supporting a friend through this very transition into entrepreneurship. The money was stuck and the doubt about her choices were hovering, but the question set her free. Amazingly, when we chatted, she didn't think she was risk averse at all, but having the bravery to leave her job in the first place told a different story.

9

PEOPLE VS. RELATIONSHIPS

I'm going to end this book on a cliché, "no man is an island," the famous words by poet, John Donne. Throughout this book, the process has been an internal discovery of self and the relationship with you, your dreams, your business and your money. Manifesting all those things, no matter how passionate you are, will amount to nothing, if you don't develop your energetic relationship skills with others. At no point did I say that money and success magically appear in your life. I reiterate that it energetically appears, which I'm more than happy to refer to as miracles at times. Diego was a young entrepreneur, taking over his father's struggling business and trying to understand the concept of holistic entrepreneurship.

He was as unaware of the impact of shifting his energy as I was, because I was also in the space of struggling when he approached me for some personal guidance. Being a sceptic, but turning to any help he could, he did what I initially ask of anyone. Simply open yourself up to the belief that anything is possible. He asked me how to do that and I told him to decide. Yes, simply decide. We chatted over coffee and he questioned the process of deciding, but there isn't one. It took him a while to understand that sometimes we need to simply make a choice to do something differently, even if we don't know what that difference is going to be. Life will present many situations to you and with a conscious mind, react differently.

Days passed and work came in and Diego became sceptical once again. He demanded to see a difference in his financial situation, and I felt his personal panic at the fear of losing his father's business. Honestly, I didn't know what else to do but wait and see because I was in very much the same space as he was. We both sat with empty pockets and baskets full of dreams. There is no dread quite like the end of a month for an entrepreneur and the dreaded phone call came from the bank. They needed payment or the full amount would be called in. Diego didn't have it, but he did manage to buy a few days and had a defining moment of vulnerability where he did what he hadn't done before. He dropped the veil of pride and crumbled in the face of his friends. It wasn't his intention to do so, but he couldn't mask his fears any longer, even if he tried. Alcohol flowed one night and as he let his guard down, he did something different. He shared his story of financial strain and lack of work, culminating in the fears of losing something his father had taken years to build. The industry he was in had been struggling, but he knew his passion was linked to continuing the family business.

Diego knew there was nothing else he wanted to do with his life's purpose and the vulnerability showed for all his tough friends to see. The rest of that evening, more of them shared their stories of struggle and what started as a boys' night out ended as a networking and brainstorming session that landed Diego work the next morning. Another friend loaned him enough money to pay to the bank, which he never would have dreamed of asking for. When we chatted a few days later, he told me it was a miracle. I'm all for miracles, but I'm more about energetic relationships and universal rewards, which is Diego's exact story.

If you have a book saying never mix business and pleasure, I give you permission to bury it. Seriously, give it right back to nature and let the pages have some purpose, because teaching entrepreneurs or anyone in business to separate their lives into compartments is not one of them. Well, it may have been, before technology became core to our existence, but I still don't understand why. I remember being taught, in secretarial college, to remain professional and leave your personal life at home. I also remember it being the toughest time in my young adult life. My father had been in Russia for nearly a year, trying to salvage a deal that had turned bad. He took a loan on our home, having been assured that it was a done deal. When he got to the other side, the story was dramatically different and literally set up a temporary home in order to fight for everything he owned.

While he hunted for anyone out there to buy the stock, he had purchased for the business deal, I was being taught to paint on a smile and stick to business. When I got to my first job, it was a totally different story. Working for my former college principal, now boss, presented me with a working environment where she let me into her world and her struggle to have a baby. Her husband was a much younger man, who also worked for the company and I got to know them both. Still hiding the majority of my woes, I empathised with her sad days and rejoiced with her on the day she finally fell pregnant. There were the traumatic ones when she feared she wouldn't carry full term, all the while carrying on being my boss and making sure we all got our jobs done.

Although my stint in corporate didn't last very long, I kept in contact with my immediate boss and with my former principal. I got to meet her son and celebrate more of her personal journeys. I may not have called her a friend, but my former boss had allowed me into her life enough to transform the way I would be a boss in the future. Almost ten years after I left her employment, we still shared a hello and checked in on each other's lives. Tragically, in 1998, I received a call saying she had been killed in a car accident. I remember sitting among people I hadn't seen in years, all weeping together, for a boss who wasn't aware of the profound impact she had made on all of us, simply by being human.

My business partner and I began as much more than that. It was only after a few years of discovering the somewhat cheesy, but very strong bond of best friendship, that we decided we would also make excellent business partners. There are endless warnings about that too and although our business has pushed the friendship to unimaginable limits, we have defied the rules. It's because those rules are based on bias and perception. The power of choice is the entrepreneurial rule breaker, making every situation unique because you choose it to be. Energy within relationships can be spoken about as the norm, because of the collective unconscious explained in chapter two. There will be thousands of stories telling of the repeated failings of business relationships, but those will fit into the unconscious majority, which you and I strive not to be. The other side of relationships within business is one of intuitively and instinctively selecting people who you can be human with. The layers of vulnerability that peel away at your emotions when embarking on entrepreneurship are never ending. Ego and Soul are constantly at loggerheads and the people in your life will inevitably become pawns in your game of success or failure.

When money is added to the mix of friendship, working with family or partnering with an acquaintance, the dynamic can easily fall into the statistic of mistrust and betrayal. Trusting another person with your financial wellbeing has nothing to do with the other person. Take into consideration the purpose of your intuition and take responsibility for the choices you made about who you chose to share your business with. This may sound extremely cynical, but I am speaking from the experience of being in partnership for over twenty years. I chose both really well, and yes, I take full responsibility for choosing them and I hope in return they praise themselves for choosing me. We were both friends before and although my first business fell to pieces and so did that friendship, I still take full responsibility for who I decided to work with.

If you are starting out in business or if you have been burned along the way, work on taking the holistic approach to choosing who you do business with. This doesn't only apply to partnership, but to employing staff and working with clients. Social media has dramatically changed the way we do business and by the time someone has decided there is potential to work with or for you, or are keen to acquire your services, they have already stalked you online. While we are busy focusing on the professional tone of our LinkedIn profile, because that is the business network after all, they have tracked you down on Facebook and discovered the more intimate you. If that scares you and you plan to stop reading any further until you have tightened your privacy settings, think again.

In 2008 I was a struggling entrepreneur who latched onto the pastime of playing around on social media. Myspace had fallen off the wagon and I was a slow starter to the Facebook craze, which was slowly being whispered through my friendship circles. I was in the phase of trying anything to get the word out about our newly born business, Lifeology, but then Facebook really was all about the sharing of posts with friends. It was so long ago that Facebook still began every status with "is" and we were forced to creatively begin every sentence of our online existence with, "Jodene is ...". I managed to share updates on snippets of my manifestation myths, but still relied heavily on my newsletter database, which wasn't significant at all.

I will never forget the day in early February 2009, when a high school friend of mine, who had emigrated to Ireland, sent me a Facebook message basically telling me to get a life. He told me to check out Twitter, which was a social network hardly noticed by South Africans at that time. It didn't take me long to find my new time-consuming obsession. Within weeks I had learned the ability to use 140 characters to connect, network and interact with fascinating people. Being slower on the uptake of many technology and online waves, South Africans were jumping on Facebook, while I was riding Twitter's rapid pace and became one of the handful of people to be active on it in South Africa.

I fiercely pursued networking my way through whoever would engage with me internationally and learned the tricks of openly chatting. 'Following first' was advice that was given to me by a young British start-up guy. He was one of many incredibly helpful people who willingly shared any knowledge about online networking that he thought I could use, and I attempted to absorb and use it all. Making myself transparent, networking first, being courteous and generous in my communication were the lessons I carried with me while I made headway to being one of the most followed South Africans on Twitter, by early 2010.

The golden rule to holistic entrepreneurship in the online space is the mindset that you never know where opportunity lies. Your online life really is like a box of chocolates and being too picky can have you overlooking some secretly great connections while you hunt down something too isolated. It was true in 2009 and it's still true today, that opening yourself up to being real and engaging with an openly trusting energy has the ability to attract some very powerful and helpful people into your life.

Had I not followed as many people as possible first, I would not have been noticed by some key individuals in the fast booming world of social media. It is now seven years since the birth of Lifeology and we have not spent a penny on advertising. I have never printed a flyer to hand out, taken a street pole ad, paid for an advertorial in a local newspaper or a slot on the local community radio station. Chat Factory is currently at the point where we have to staff up for a third time because we are at capacity, with me having daily requests for information on our social media service offering. Lifeology is doing equally well, with Greg fully booked with his time, all through people we have networked and connected with online. We both have a dozen stories of first engaging with people on an intimately personal level before being offered the opportunity of work.

One of the most supportive networks in my circle, who is high up in the corporate ladder, invited me to tea because I had boasted so much about my love for it. Another read my bio, which stated that I believe ice cream solves all the world's problems. He Tweeted me back to say he had to prove if the theory was true and after numerous bowls of ice cream through the years, he has become one of the most prominent mouthpieces about my online social services. We have never done business together, but he doesn't need to have worked with me to be absorbed into the transparency of who I am, online and off.

All I have guided you through in this book is weaved into any online and personal connections with your world around you. Relationship building is vital for entrepreneurship. It is also the most openly intuitive process you will go through in the process of becoming a successful businessperson. Even if your business is heavily product-based and your interaction with people is limited, the handful of people you need will either make or break your success story. We are trained to hire on skill and qualification, which works well if you are employing a doctor or tradesman. For the majority, we should be using our intuition to see who would fit well into the dynamic of our business. My mother taught me this when I was deputy principal of the beauty college. She prided herself in being able to pick out who had the tenacity for beauty therapy, despite the high marks or school merits. It wasn't a formula she could teach me, but watching her chat to the promising students and seeing her draw out their potential passion for their industry was a priceless business lesson. Don't hire on skill because that can be taught. Hire on passion. The passion doesn't have to be for the job, but it must be woven into the story of their lives. I have met accountants who are passionate about numbers and heads of HR who thrive on the development of people, so yes, we all need the energetic ignition of passion and purpose.

The same applies for the selection of your client base. Don't kid yourself into believing you will be a financial success merely because you will say yes to every person or company that needs your services. Providing services to energy-sapping clients is more detrimental to the flow of your business than letting your own negativity and fears get in the way. Do you remember the emphasis on fun in chapter five's process of finding business faith? If your energetic relationships are not fun, then it is impossible for it not to filter through your business. Clients are not merely the provider of money for your business. They are demanding on your time and users of your energy, both of which are vital for daily survival. If you are being occupied by thrilling hours you put into the joint passion you share for a client, then keep going and the rewards will pay off. However, if you are feeling emotionally drained by the negative energy of an individual or company who you are providing a service to, I strongly suggest you reassess the business arrangement.

The longstanding business rule which applies to all of us is to not put our eggs in one basket. Although we are taught this, because there is the expectation of the client moving on from our services, we never account for our need to move on from the client. Relationships are the same, whether it is friendship, marriage or business. Remaining in a toxic relationship will poison all the apples in the basket and most people stay because they put everything, they have into that one relationship and can't get out. I often share my story of firing a Chat Factory client for the first time. We were a small team, consisting of myself and one employee, with four clients all needing full social media services. They were the smallest in fees in their requirement, but they were also the most demanding. Akin to a yapping miniature dachshund, barking instructions constantly and drowning out the time we needed for the larger, higher paying clients, I watched as my one staff member grew weary. Ensuring the people who work for you are happy is as much your responsibility as it is theirs and this one was not happy.

Behind the scenes, I worked at securing more work to cover the upcoming shortfall and I also assured my employee that I was aware of the struggle to deal with the negative energy the client was bringing into our work environment. I'm a firm believer in calculated risk, but also know the universe conspires to swiftly assist you as soon as you have made a decision in your highest esteem. Within a few months of knowing the energetic damage the client could do to my business, I had replaced the equal income I needed with other work. One Monday, after posting approved content to their Facebook page, the client went in and changed the working of their post, showing gross mistrust in my employee's capabilities and I turned to him and asked him if he was having fun working on the client's account. His response was a blatant no, but he did what most employees do and promised he would continue to work on it, because that is what employees are expected to do.

Holistically, that is absolutely untrue. Employees are an extension of your energetic pulse through the business and if they are justly unhappy, you stand by them and make the necessary changes, just as you would if you were operating in your highest esteem as a solo service provider. If you are and this relates directly to you, then ask yourself if you are having fun working with the ones who are transferring their money, which is pure energy, to you. With secured future work, I called for a meeting with the client and gave notice of non-renewal contract.

Remaining in integrity is vital for business, so giving fair warning and assuring them I would assist with a replacement agency is the thread that still holds the relationship I have with my now ex client. I continue to offer my advice, because that should always be free, and they graciously acknowledge that I did what was best for all of us. Subsequently, they took my advice and hired internally, where their employee has my number on speed dial as they constantly grow into their position of in-house social media manager.

The other side of relationship building is allowing the client to personally bond with you and your world. With the online world crawling with at least a handful of people offering the same services as any of us, it has very much returned to the intimate connections past generations grew up with. You would think it would have become more clinical and the one with the fairest price would win, but that ship has sailed and carried many people's hard earned money along with it. This may have always been true for smaller business, but there is a definite trend in the corporate world also wanting more bonding for their buck. One of my clients is a large international company and instructions are filtered down from Europe for local implementation. Slowly, as the economy has begun to weaken worldwide, the European office chose to tighten their belts and called for a consolidation of all smaller businesses into one through-the-line agency for marketing, public relations and online. Myself and two other entrepreneurs risked losing our largest clients. At the time, the company was generating eighty percent of the business's income. Yet, myself and one of the entrepreneurs witnessed something remarkable. The South African division fought back relentlessly.

For nearly three months, the two of us would call each other to calm the panic for the day. We swayed between knowing we had done something so right to talking about what our next step would be if our retainer fell away. With each passing day, we continued to supply the business services we passionately provided to the client. This uncertainty fell over the December festive season, which was filled with mixed emotions for all of us and our New Year's wishes between client and business spoke of a business lesson I will always live by. The head of marketing wrote on my Facebook wall because yes, she is my Facebook friend. She wished me a happy new year and publicly promised me that she wasn't done fighting for us to continue working together. By the end of January, South Africa was one of the only countries in the company to have overturned the international request for a through the line agency.

Months later, when on a roadshow with my client, she told me that I had opened myself up and let them in, not as a company but as individuals who were passionate about their industry. She confessed to the appreciation of seeing the inside of my world through my Facebook activities and knowing that I was often referring to the high point of my day as hours I had spent at my client. Wishing them for their birthday and arriving with a bottle of bubbly to celebrate one of their successes, set Chat Factory aside from the rest. A few years back, my family was held up in an armed robbery, which traumatised all of us. If I had listened to the business advice I was given by the white-collar world, I would not have walked into that meeting and allowed my vulnerability to show. We spent the first half hour talking about similar traumas and clients became fellow human beings, who in turn entrust their online presence to me knowing there are bigger agencies out there who have a stronger work force, but would bring their corporate old school mentality too.

In hiring of staff and increasing my employee base, I have adopted the same principles. I am amazed by the number of people who still reiterate that employees should not be let into your personal space in the social online circles. Sure, if Facebook is strictly private due to the online protection of young children, I get that. There are other platforms or settings that we don't utilise enough in the Facebook space, but energetically not allowing your team in is going to productively keep them out.

Although I agree with the rule that it is not necessary to go partying with your staff, I believe strongly in allowing them to see inside of your world. It is more important that you see inside of theirs. Don't be the boss who doesn't know or care if your employee's child is having a sick day. Take them to lunch on their birthday and have an open door policy for real life stresses and fears. We banter on about loyalty fading away in marriages and intimate relationships, but they are equally at risk in the business world. Without respectful relationships with clients, employees and the world around you, you run the risk of isolating yourself from the unique way of holistically running a business. Doing this differently to the rest of the world weighs heavily on standing out as a handful of people who have time for other people in this technology driven world. Be the one who sets yourself apart from all the rest, by trusting the power of relating on an intimate and human level. That's where the money lies.

Most probably the toughest part of relationships with people lies in the depths you can go in your relationship with yourself. There is this untruth that vulnerability has no place in the workspace. Which might have been true for older generation, but the more we become heart centred and know that our heads don't send us in the direction of our highest potential, the more emotional we naturally become. Being vulnerable means allowing yourself to speak your truth, within a safe space which you create for yourself. If you spend your working life waiting for others to create that space for you, the wall may never come down. There is so much to the shifting energy between teams and relationships with those who you have a 'transactional' relationship with, and the foundation lies in this raw quality.

As this is the second edition of the book, a few years have passed since I put all the pieces together and completed it. Reflecting to when I wrote it and remembering there were tough financial times, I see myself back in the same space. This can't be a coincidence. What is money trying to each me? If you go back to chapter on money, Self-Worth vs Financial-Worth, you will know that we are always supported by the universe, to move in the direction of our highest esteem. Money shows up as a great voice when we don't have the courage, strength or confidence to find our own strong voice. When financial discussions need to be had, there is no greater time to need to rely on vulnerability. This is not a lesson I learned overnight. I first had to go through depths of doubt. In my passion, my joy, my ability to be a boss and in myself. I am not an island in my entrepreneurial journey. I have a supportive and encouraging business partner and a dedicated team of staff. However, the moment I needed to rely on my courage to be vulnerable, I retraced, and it felt safer to be dwelling in doubt, than having honest conversations, which started and ended with, "I don't know."

I didn't speak to Greg through the whole of December and my staff have recently told me they felt my insecurity, which in-turn made them feel insecure too. I could literally feel the stability of my self-worth uprooting itself. I know it's humanly impossible, but I was so intrenched in fear and uncertainty, that I was energetically putting myself in determent. Standing on the grass, deep in awareness, all I had the wisdom to do was feel my roots deep in the group, even though I couldn't remember much of what made me worthy.

I could have gone on like this for months. My business might have taken more knocks than it has been feeling, but there was a tiny voice which kept encouraging me to be vulnerable. Start with my business partner and show him that the courage and never say die attitude which he always reminds me of, was hard for me to tap into. It took that first step of vulnerability, on both our parts, for the spark to ignite and money to remind that when I show up, it will show up too.

The next step was a much tougher one. Having to be vulnerable with people who rely on you for their financial wellbeing is most probably the toughest part of being a business owner for me. I don't have it in me to say I'm simply their boss and I'm not responsible for their happiness. When you take on the responsibility to trade financially and energetically with someone, with integrity, you do become responsible to each other. My team have never let me down on their side of the bargain. Even when it's been frustrating and the energy between us has not been aligned, they have showed up. It took me a few days to pluck up the courage, but it was my turn to show up too. In the most important way. To be vulnerable and connect them with as the unit we are. Speaking my truth, with tons of passion, but still being honest that there is uncertainty in the air. Allowing the dialogue to open, so they had the opportunity to be more than just the team who serves our clients. I could see it allowing them to become an integral part of the engine which keeps the business going. We spoke for hours and then turned that talk into a strategy session, to re-imagine what it looks like to all create opportunities for the energy of our business to shift. Even that was vulnerable for me. I am used to holding full responsibility for finding the clients, presenting to potential clients and putting all the pieces in place for the service we offer to provide. To hear my team say they wanted to be part of the process was a mix of concern that I was not getting it right and the gratitude that they saw their ability to contribute, and therefore shift into their own level of responsibility. It hasn't taken me long to feel myself settle and hold myself in high esteem for braving a conversation which I admittedly had been avoiding. I believe all the universe, money and life waits for moments like this, from all of us.

AFTERWORD

As an entrepreneur, it is vital to keep yourself in check with all levels of relationships and coming full circle, the one that counts the most is with yourself. Although the world is filled with the do's and don'ts of business practice, it is not filled with enough of the personal reliance on self-discovery as your compass to success.

Go consciously into the world of business and as cliché as possible, dance to the beat of your own drum. Do not conform to the manuscript of those who have gone before you. Do walk in your own steps of business faith. Remain conscious and let happiness be your guide. Treat money and people with the same nurturing, but mostly have fun.

I wish you abundance!

ACKNOWLEDGMENTS

This book has been a lifetime in the making and has taken me on personal journey of realisation, as each chapter unfolded. It was a stark reminder that happiness and choice are the cornerstone of any success story.

Although my successes are all self-actualised, I would not be the businesswoman I am today and this book would still be a dream, if it were not for some very special people.

To my business partner and best friend, Greg Arthur, for teaching me the greatest lessons about integrity, trust and my unearthed abilities. Thank you for your unfailing belief in me and in us. Thank you for loving me enough to tell me when it's time to get over myself and just get published.

To my dad, who would have first found a spelling error and then been wildly proud of me. Thank you for leaving me with the legacy of never ever thinking small and no detail was too irrelevant.

To my mom, who has been my entrepreneurial icon since I was a little girl and is still working, when others her age have long retired. Mom, you took me under your wing and unconditionally loved and supported me, even when you weren't quite sure if I knew where I was heading.

To my dear friend and writing coach, Shelley Pembroke Hartman, who held back my fears while I wrote each chapter. Shells, your strict deadlines and truly compassionate guidance is the reason this book is a reality today.

To my amazing family, friends and people in my world who unfailingly support me.

Thank you!

Jodene.

ABOUT THE AUTHOR

Jodene Shaer is an entrepreneur at heart; writer and speaker by passion. She is a strategist and advisor to individuals, businesses and brands, facilitating change both online and off. Through her online social presence, she openly demonstrates what a life of courage, consciousness and a sense of humour looks like. She is a dedicated business partner, with a holistic approach to entrepreneurship, money and success.

Jodene began her entrepreneurial path in 2000 and after closing two businesses in the beauty industry, in 2008 she co-founded a people development business, Lifeology with her current business partner, Greg Arthur. Greg is based in the UK, which has taken their businesses to international heights.

Through sharing her philosophies, she was recognised for her natural talent in the social media world and 2012, co-founded Chat Factory. Specialising in South African and International social media strategy, content and community management and influencer marketing, alongside her team, she is South African Chief Executive and head strategist.

She was a 2012 finalist in the South Africa Rising Star Awards for Entrepreneurship and in the social media space, is often called upon by media as a Twitter expert in line with breaking news.

Jodene lives in Johannesburg, South Africa with an office anywhere philosophy for both businesses, enabling her to travel the world and continuously expand her holistic approach to business and life.

www.ingramcontent.com/pod-product-compliance
Ingram Content Group UK Ltd.
Pitfield, Milton Keynes, MK11 3LW, UK
UKHW021053270726
13967UKWH00012B/637